A Moment in God's Word

A 52 Week Devotional

A Moment in God's Word

A 52 Week Devotional

Stephen N. Rummage

NORTHEASTERN BAPTIST PRESS

A Moment in God's Word
A 52 Week Devotional
Copyright © 2023 by Stephen N. Rummage
Edited by Kim Jackson and Noah Graves
Published by Northeastern Baptist Press
Post Office Box 4600
Bennington, VT 05201

Cover design by Leason Stiles

Paperback ISBN: 978-1-953331-22-9

FROM THE PUBLISHER

Through several syndicated radio networks, *Moving Forward* and *Moving Forward Minute with Dr. Stephen Rummage* are heard daily across the United States. Dr. Rummage communicates biblical truth in a profound, yet simple style. With clarity, high energy, and humor, his messages enable listeners to understand God's Word and move forward in their relationship with Jesus Christ. Dr. Rummage's messages can also be heard via his webpage, www.MovingForwardRadio.org and through his *Moving Forward App* available for both iPhone and Android.

Dr. Rummage serves as the Senior Pastor of Quail Springs Baptist Church in Oklahoma City, and has pastored churches in Florida, North Carolina, Virginia, and Louisiana. He has served on the faculty of three seminaries including Southeastern Baptist Theological Seminary, New Orleans Baptist Theological Seminary, and Midwestern Baptist Theological Seminary. In addition, he is a sought after Bible conference speaker and author of several books.

In this volume Dr. Rummage brings clear, concise, and consistent encouragement to continually move forward in your relationship with Jesus Christ through a 52-week daily devotional. Each day the reader will be encouraged in their walk with Jesus, as Dr. Rummage communicates a passage of Scripture, illustrates a biblical truth, and practically applies God's Word to real life. Each devotional concludes with a prayer based on the day's text. *A Moment in God's Word* will no doubt prove encouraging and transforming in the reader's daily life.

A Moment in God's Word has been designed in such a way as to enable you to begin benefitting from this daily devotional any time of year. The book is built around a 52-week layout, allowing you to be encouraged from the first day the book arrives. You may choose to start in Week 1 and proceed for 52 weeks, or you may choose to begin with the week of the year that the book comes into your possession. Either way, you are in for an exciting year of moving forward in your relationship with the Lord through the aid of Dr. Rummage's insights.

Having been blessed to know Dr. Rummage for many years and having served with him in various capacities, it is my great pleasure to publish this work and commend it to you. I am confident that whether you are just beginning to explore a relationship with Jesus, a young believer, or someone who has walked with Jesus for many years, you will be encouraged and you will grow closer to our amazing Lord as you include these readings in your daily walk.

In Him,

Mark H. Ballard
President, NEBC
Publisher, NEBP

SUNDAY

For your name's sake, O Lord,
pardon my guilt, for it is great.
Psalm 25:11

Michele and I love watching television programs that feature distressed houses being fixed up and flipped. But I've noticed this: the stars of those shows never seem to come across a property that's beyond help. In fact, the worse the house is "before," the more amazed we are by how it looks "after" the fixer-uppers have worked their magic.

God reveals His highest glory in redeeming us from our deepest sin. No job is too hard for God. He will never declare that anyone is too sinful to come to Christ. The greater our sin appears, the more amazingly His grace saves!

Father, I praise You for redeeming me from my sin!
Thank You for transforming my life by Your grace.

Monday

Therefore, if anyone is in Christ, he is a new creation.
The old has passed away; behold, the new has come.
2 Corinthians 5:17

Yearly, six hundred thousand Americans have heart bypass surgery. Doctors counsel these patients about how to change their lifestyle so that the bypass results are successful. Eat a healthy diet. Quit smoking. Exercise. Get rid of stress. And you know what? Ninety percent of heart bypass patients foolishly return to their old lifestyle that nearly killed them.

Jesus Christ gives every believer a brand-new heart and life. It would be foolish to return toour old sinful lifestyle that caused your spiritual death! If Jesus Christ has saved you, then guard your new heart by obeying everything He says. That will ensure a healthy life that honors Him.

Lord Jesus, I am so thankful for the new life that You've given me. Give me grace today to live, not focusing on old things that You saved me from, but on Your new work in me.

Tuesday

Stay dressed for action and keep your lamps burning.
Luke 12:35

Severe weather emergencies like snowstorms and tornadoes are very common where we live. Michele reminds me regularly to keep my cell phone charged. We don't want to have a twenty-five percent charge when the power goes out. And you can count on it: in Oklahoma, where the wind really does go sweeping down the plain, the power will go out.

Here's something else you can count on: Jesus Christ is going to come back! Jesus says that a wise servant will get ready and stay ready for his master to return, because he doesn't know when it will be. The return of Jesus Christ will catch you by surprise, but don't let it catch you unprepared! So, get ready and stay ready, because Jesus is coming!

Lord Jesus, help me to be prepared for Your return. I want to live ready to see You when You appear!

WEDNESDAY

*And be like men who are waiting for their master to
come home from the wedding feast, so that they may
open the door to him at once when he comes and knocks.*

Luke 12:36

Legendary basketball coach Dean Smith is famous for his game-winning strategy called the four corners. When his team led late in the game, instead of running plays to keep scoring, they just passed from corner to corner until the game ended. It made for very boring games. Later the league benched the four corners by instituting the shot clock. When time's counting down, players ignore the status quo, and they play the game!

God's Word says that there's a shot clock on the world as well as on your life. When time runs out, you will give an account to Jesus for how you've played the game. Don't just maintain your life's status quo, humming along in the world and living to please yourself. Let's faithfully serve our Lord Jesus Christ until our time runs out.

---

*Father, whether in death or at Your return, one day I will see
You face to face. I want You to find me faithful when my time
on earth is done!*

THURSDAY

Which of you by being anxious can add
a single hour to his span of life?
Luke 12:25

Imagine a fog, one hundred feet thick, covering about seven city blocks. Scientists tell us that if you condensed every droplet of water in that fog, you'd have only enough water to fill one drinking glass. Fog is actually a little bit of water blown all out of proportion. When that happens, that little amount of water becomes dangerous and distracting.

Worry is like fog. Worry magnifies small things so that they appear bigger and bigger. Worry is productive – it produces all kinds of problems – in our thoughts, in our emotions, and in our health. But worry can never ever make things better! So instead of worrying, bring your cares to Jesus. You are valuable to Him, and He promises to take care of you.

Lord God, I believe that You are more powerful than anything
that worries me. Lord, I trust You to take care of me today.

FRIDAY

*Do not be anxious about anything, but in everything
by prayer and supplication with thanksgiving let your
requests be made known to God.*
Philippians 4:6

A man hurrying through an airport zoomed past a guy dressed in a uniform. The uniformed man asked him, "Where are you in such a hurry to get to?" The man said, "I'm trying to get to the gate for flight such-and-such to such-and-such city." The uniformed man smiled and said, "Well I'm the pilot on that flight; I promise it won't leave until I get there. Just calm down and walk with me. You'll get where you need to be on time."

If the pilot is not panicked, you don't need to panic! When Jesus Christ is the captain of your life, you don't need to be anxious or worry. Instead, calm down and walk with Jesus. He'll meet your needs and get you where you need to be at just the right time.

---

*Father, thank You for inviting me to tell You what I need and
for promising to take care of me. Help me to be thankful today
instead of anxious.*

SATURDAY

*Each one must give as he has decided in his heart,
not reluctantly or under compulsion, for God loves a
cheerful giver.*
2 Corinthians 9:7

My parents taught me to tithe when I was young. I watched my dad write his tithe check week after week. However, I never got the impression that tithing was a religious duty. In fact, I'll never forget my dad's words: "Stephen, I'm giving this, not because I have to, but because I love Jesus."

That's the attitude God is looking for in His people. You can give without loving. The Pharisees were A+ tithers, but they got an F in love. They gave because their religion said they had to. But if you really love the Lord, you'll give to Him generously and cheerfully. God loves and abundantly blesses that kind of giving.

Lord Jesus, thank You that you are generous to me because you love me. Please help me to give generously with a happy heart for all You've done for me.

SUNDAY

Therefore, since we have been justified by faith, we have peace with God through our Lord Jesus Christ.

Romans 5:1

A page in a children's book called *I Can Do it Myself*[1] says this:

> *I can ride,*
>
> *I can hide,*
>
> *I can reach a high shelf.*
>
> *Hey, look at me!*
>
> *I can do it myself!"*

Those are really great accomplishments when you're four years old.

But to be right with God, you can't do it yourself! None of our religious deeds are acceptable to God for our salvation. But you can be made right with God through His Son, Jesus Christ! He died on the cross to pay for your sins, and He rose from the dead to give you eternal life. Jesus Christ has done everything you need to be right with God.

Father, I admit that I can't save myself. I am so grateful that You saw my helplessness and came to my rescue by sending Jesus to die for me.

[1]*I Can Do It Myself,* by Stephen Krensky

MONDAY

Nothing is covered up that will not be revealed,
or hidden that will not be known.
Luke 12:2

When our son Joshua was a teenager, I asked him, "Son, am I the same guy at church that I am at home?" He said, "You're louder and more interesting at church than at home." I said, "Am I funnier at church than at home?" He said, "You're not funny at church or at home." Okay, I gave him that one. I said, "Am I the same guy in public that I am at home with you and mom?" He said, "Yeah, Dad. You are." I was relieved.

Are you the same at home as you are at church on Sunday? Let me ask it another way: are you the same at church as you are at home, Monday through Saturday? Our families are negatively impacted spiritually by hypocrisy. Let's commit to be people of godly integrity for the sake of our families, so that we do everything possible to make Jesus Christ attractive to them.

Lord, search my heart and show me where I might be living
hypocritically. Help me to live with integrity so my life brings
praise to Jesus wherever I am.

TUESDAY

Therefore do not pronounce judgment before the time, before the Lord comes, who will bring to light the things now hidden in darkness and will disclose the purposes of the heart. Then each one will receive his commendation from God.
1 Corinthians 4:5

In the early days of television there was a long-running program called *I've Got a Secret*. Guests came on that show to play a game where their secrets would be exposed. Now, their secrets were fun and harmless. It hurt no one for their secrets to be revealed. But many people play dangerous games with secret sins that they never want found out.

Everything that's hidden eventually comes to light. And one day God will expose every secret sin under the light of His judgment. Secret sin that promises to be sweet and private often winds up being bitter and public. Holy integrity in your secret life will protect you from being painfully exposed in sin and hypocrisy. Always remember: God knows your heart.

———————————

Lord, I don't want to live in fear of secrets being exposed in my life. Empower me to be careful to watch over my own life so that I am unashamed of the secret places of my heart.

WEDNESDAY

Therefore whatever you have said in the dark shall be heard in the light, and what you have whispered in private rooms shall be proclaimed on the housetops.

Luke 12:3

Astronomers tell us that one side of the moon always faces the earth, and the other side is always turned away. We sometimes call that side the dark side of the moon. But the truth is, the sun's light reaches both sides of the moon. None of the moon is hidden from the sun's light.

Mark Twain said that "like the moon, we all have a dark side we don't want anyone to see." There is no darkness where you can hide from God. If your inside doesn't match your outside, stop pretending. Jesus Christ is the light of the world, who died for your sin to rescue you from darkness. Don't live in hypocrisy. Instead, come to Jesus and live in His light.

Lord Jesus, please shine Your light in every corner of my heart. Show me anything that needs to be cleaned up. I want my life – my thoughts and intentions – to always be pleasing to You.

Thursday

*For his anger is but for a moment, and his favor
is for a lifetime. Weeping may tarry for the night,
but joy comes with the morning.*

Psalm 30:5

Grief is the sadness we feel from losing something or someone important to us. But not everyone's grief journey is the same. Someone has said that grief is not like a spiral; it's not that organized. Someone else said that grief is like a thumbprint. Each person's grief is a unique experience. Regardless, all grief is hard.

Your grief is unique to you. There's no schedule. But God knows you perfectly. He understands your grief perfectly. He will not leave you alone in your grief. He enters into the process of your grief, and He will bring you through it.

----

*Lord God, I'm so thankful for Your promise that the hurt,
pain, and tears of my loss won't last forever. I look forward
to experiencing Your joy once more.*

FRIDAY

Yes, we are of good courage, and we would rather be away from the body and at home with the Lord.
2 Corinthians 5:8

I was recently driving through Oklahoma City when a car really caught my eye. It had a Hawaii license plate! That license plate had the word *Aloha* on it. There was even a bumper sticker on the back of the car that said, *I love Maui*. And here's what I thought: they had relocated from Hawaii to Oklahoma. They had even relocated their car! But they hadn't relocated their loyalties.

When you get saved, the kingdom of God becomes your home. But sometimes we keep our Earth bumper sticker. The great challenge of the Christian life is to overcome divided loyalties and to fully identify with God's kingdom. Remember: Heaven is not only your eternal home; it's your better and more desirable home!

Lord Jesus, I can't wait to see Heaven; but more than that, I can't wait to see You! Thank You for preparing that new home for me so I can be there with You forever.

Saturday

If then you have been raised with Christ,
seek the things that are above, where Christ is,
seated at the right hand of God.
Colossians 3:1

When I visit the beach, I almost always see beach-combers with metal detectors, scanning the sands for hidden treasure. It's all they think about. They don't watch the waves, or the people walking by. Their attention is constantly focused downward, seeking that treasure.

If you're saved, don't keep looking down for treasure. Look up! Heaven is your real home. In fact, it's much more real than what you are experiencing here! Every day, let heaven become more and more important to you. Though it's hidden for now, one day you will see the vast treasure waiting for you where Jesus is. So, look up today, and set your heart on heaven and on Jesus.

Father, You are my greatest treasure. Nothing I have here,
no matter how shiny or beautiful, can ever compare with
what You have awaiting me in heaven.

Sunday

And to put on the new self, created after the likeness
of God in true righteousness and holiness.
Ephesians 4:24

When I was a kid, my mom always bought my clothes about four sizes too big. She'd roll up my pants legs, cuff my sleeves, and cinch my pants at the waist so they wouldn't slide off me. I'd say, "Mom, these clothes don't fit!" She'd answer, "It's alright. You'll grow." Well, she was right. I always grew into my too big clothes.

When you get saved, Jesus gives you brand new clothes. In the beginning they're too big. His holiness and His righteousness that we're to put on, are much bigger than our sinfulness. But you put them on by faith, and His grace will empower you to grow into them.

Father, thank You for providing me a perfect new wardrobe to match my new life in Jesus Christ. By Your grace, I will wear my "new self" so that people will know that I am Yours.

Monday

For neither circumcision counts for anything, nor un-circumcision, but a new creation.

Galatians 6:15

Every year Michele and I like to compare last year's photo Christmas cards from friends to the new ones. Once we got a card and recognized everyone in the new picture, except the husband! The guy in the new photo weighed much less and had an updated hair style. He didn't wear glasses, and he dressed stylishly. We finally agreed: this wasn't a different person, just an update of our old friend!

That's not how it works when you get saved. Jesus doesn't just update your life. He makes you a brand new person! The new you is made to grow into the likeness of Jesus Christ. So, live today like the new person Jesus has made you.

Father, thank You for the new creation that You have made me. Help me to use new words, thoughts, and actions to match the new person that I am in Jesus Christ.

TUESDAY

This was according to the eternal purpose that he has realized in Christ Jesus our Lord, in whom we have boldness and access with confidence through our faith in him.

Ephesians 3:11-12

Wisdom says that it's unsafe to use one password for all your online activities. Using the same password for everything you do puts you at a high level of risk. You should have a unique password for every account.

However, the opposite is true spiritually. You need only one password to access God, and it's the same for everyone. The only password you need is the blood of His Son Jesus Christ. Only through the blood of Christ can you access God's salvation, His forgiveness, His comfort, and the presence of His Holy Spirit. The blood of Jesus is your all access pass to the things of God. It is a secure access that can never be breached.

Lord God, it is amazing that I have access to You, the Creator of the universe through Your Son Jesus. Thank You for the blood of Jesus that makes me able to come into Your presence.

WEDNESDAY

Therefore say to the house of Israel, "Thus says the Lord GOD: 'Repent and turn away from your idols, and turn away your faces from all your abominations.'"
Ezekiel 14:6

My grandfather worked at an aluminum processing plant. That plant operated twenty-four hours a day, seven days a week, every day of the year. They didn't even take off for Christmas or Thanksgiving. That factory was constantly producing. They never stopped.

The notable minister John Calvin said that we continually produce idols in our own hearts. Not wood or stone images, but things that grab hold of our affections, taking the place in our hearts where only God deserves to be. Sometimes, we are blind to our idols, so we need to ask God to reveal them to us. When He does, we need to tear them down. God far surpasses any other thing we look to for satisfaction.

Father, show me what things in my life I have made into an idol. Then help me to destroy it and worship You alone.

THURSDAY

*Therefore, we are ambassadors for Christ, God
making his appeal through us. We implore you
on behalf of Christ, be reconciled to God.*
2 Corinthians 5:20

Once I asked my dad, a barber, if he would join me on a mission journey to a foreign country. I had a plan: While he cut hair, I'd share the gospel with the guy in the chair. Dad had never even been out of the United States. But he said yes! I was able to share the gospel with twenty-seven teenage boys that week as my dad cut their hair. Twenty-six of them prayed to receive Jesus Christ as Savior. I'm so glad my dad said yes to God!

We are Christ's ambassadors. When you say yes to whatever God has for you, He'll use you for His kingdom – sometimes in surprising places. Where will God use you? Say *yes* and find out!

---

*Lord Jesus, thank You for the precious opportunity to speak to
people about You and to invite them to be reconciled to God.
Help me to represent You well.*

FRIDAY

So whether we are at home or away,
we make it our aim to please him.
2 Corinthians 5:9

One day as Michele and I walked through the capital city of another country, we passed by a beautiful building, fenced in, and surrounded by a secure wall. The American flag flew inside the wall. It was the United States Embassy. In any country, the embassy is the territory of the country whose ambassador lives there. The ambassador doesn't represent himself, but the interests of the country who sends him.

The church is God's embassy on earth, and every believer is His ambassador. We have the assignment of representing Him to the world wherever we are. Wherever you are, at home or away, make it your aim to please God.

Lord Jesus, I admit that I sometimes want to please other people, and often, myself, more than I want to please You. Help me to aim to please You today and every day.

SATURDAY

And give no opportunity to the devil.
Ephesians 4:27

Recently I finished a telephone call with somebody, and as soon as I hung up, I put hand sanitizer on my hands. Michele said, "What are you doing?" I said, "You can never be too safe." Well, that was an over-reaction, but if we've learned anything during Covid, it's that unseen things are very real, and sometimes very dangerous.

The Bible teaches that Satan and his demons are very real and extremely dangerous. One of Satan's best lies is that they don't exist! Demons sow seeds of conflict and false teaching in churches. Satan works hard to trip you up and destroy your testimony. So, stay alert! Ask God to give you discernment and power to recognize and avoid Satan's schemes.

Father, give me Your grace to live today, robbing the devil of opportunities to trip me up and make me fall. Make me alert to his schemes!

SUNDAY

And do not turn aside after empty things that cannot profit or deliver, for they are empty.
1 Samuel 12:21

In 2005, NFL quarterback Tom Brady had already earned three Super Bowl rings. He said, "Why do I still think there's something greater out there for me? This can't be all it's cracked up to be." I don't know if Tom Brady has ever found what he was looking for. But not even four more Super Bowl rings could fill those empty places in his life.

You were created by Jesus Christ for Himself. Living for anything else can't profit you eternally or deliver earthly satisfaction. The greater thing we're all seeking is only found in Jesus Christ. Living your life to bring Him glory will fill your emptiness to overflowing with the satisfaction you were meant to enjoy.

Lord Jesus, I don't want to waste anymore time chasing things that leave me empty. In You alone are my satisfaction and purpose found. Help me to chase after You.

MONDAY

The Lord is not slow to fulfill his promise as some count slowness, but is patient toward you, not wishing that any should perish, but that all should reach repentance.

2 Peter 3:9

When Michele and I visited the British Museum, we saw stone carvings made by the ancient Assyrians. They portrayed themselves as viciously conquering their enemies, gouging out their eyes, cutting off their arms, and leaving them to die on the ground. They even played games with their enemy's severed heads. The Assyrians were wicked, wicked people.

Remember Jonah? Well, these were the people that God sent Jonah to preach to in Nineveh! Their sin was horrible, ugly, disturbing, and treacherous! When they heard Jonah's message, they repented, and God forgave them. There really are no limits to God's grace. You cannot out-sin God's supply of forgiveness. So, turn from your sin and come to Jesus; He wants to forgive you.

Father, I'm humbled that You forgive wicked people, including me. Search my heart, put Your finger on the sin I need to turn from, and help me to run to You for mercy and forgiveness.

Tuesday

Therefore be careful lest the light in you be darkness.
Luke 11:35

Seven-year-old Justin had just gotten saved. He had all kinds of questions about Jesus. One day he asked his mom: "Mom, Jesus is bigger than us, right?" His mom said, "Right." Justin said, "And He lives inside of Christians, right?" She said, "That's right, son." Then Justin asked a very perceptive question; he said, "Well, if Jesus is bigger than us, why doesn't He show?"

In your life, does Jesus show? Without the light of Jesus Christ, there's only darkness. If you cover up His light in your life, not even you will be able to see! Don't walk in the dark. Today, ask the Lord to show Himself in and through you, not so others see you, but so they can see Jesus.

Lord Jesus, I want You to show in my life. When others hear me speak and when they see me act, help them to see Your light shining in me.

WEDNESDAY

Since then we have a great high priest who has passed through the heavens, Jesus, the Son of God, let us hold fast our confession.

Hebrews 4:14

As a kid, when I visited my grandparents in the country, at night I slept in an old iron bed with a feather mattress. That bed was really sturdy on both ends, but it sagged badly in the middle! Let's just say that for the best night's sleep in the whole wide world, stay away from the saggy middle of a feather bed.

Sometimes Christians struggle to find confidence in the saggy middle, between getting saved and going to heaven. That space can seem unsure, but God has a solid purpose for every day of your life! Through our great high priest, God's Son Jesus Christ, He supplies His grace, mercy, strength, and joy to us for each day.

Father, until the day when I'm with You, thank You for the mercy, grace, strength, and joy You give as I walk by faith.

THURSDAY

For by grace you have been saved through faith. And this is not your own doing; it is the gift of God, not a result of works, so that no one may boast.
Ephesians 2:8-9

Many think that the greatest NFL team of all time was the 1972 Miami Dolphins. They had a fantastic coach, and many great players who contributed to their success, but analysts cite two Dolphins players from that year's team who they say contributed zero to the success of the team. But guess what? They won, too, because they were on the team.

We bring nothing to the game that contributes to our salvation. Jesus alone has done the work and won the victory. But we share in His victory because He is our great high priest. Today, He is praying for you so that you can share in the victory He has won.

Lord God, I have nothing good to give to You. I'm humbled that You share everything with me, including Your victory over sin and death.

FRIDAY

*For we do not have a high priest who is unable to
sympathize with our weaknesses, but one who in every
respect has been tempted as we are, yet without sin.*

Hebrews 4:15

Have you ever poured your heart out to someone, and though they listen, you can just tell they don't get it? Then they suddenly say something that makes you think, "You have no idea what I'm going through right now."

Jesus Christ can sympathize with all of your heartaches and pains, because He's been there. He's been tired, a hungry, and thirsty. He has been through disappointment, heartbreak, and sorrow. He's been misunderstood. He even knows what it's like to die. So, pour your heart out to Jesus; He always understands, and He's right beside you to strengthen you.

---

*Father, it's often so hard for me to identify with others'
struggles. But You completely understand every struggle I
have. I'm grateful that You never misunderstand me.*

SATURDAY

Therefore, holy brothers, you who share in a heavenly calling, consider Jesus, the apostle and high priest of our confession.
Hebrews 3:1

In recent years, personal safety has become an obsession. But there's one place where we more readily give in to a real threat to our safety, and that's in our vehicles! Distracted drivers hurt themselves and others every day! They focus on eating, drinking, texting, grooming, and finding what they dropped under the seat - distracted driving is dangerous!

Distracted living can be equally harmful. Work, politics, hobbies, and entertainment – these distractions can easily steal our attention from Jesus. We spend our time on these things that don't profit us, and find we have no time left for Jesus. Don't spend your best energy on the wrong things. The Bible says, "Consider Jesus." Don't let anything distract you from looking at Him.

———————

Lord Jesus, the many things I have to think about every day can potentially distract me from thinking about You. Help me to intentionally set my focus on You moment by moment.

SUNDAY

For whoever has entered God's rest has also rested from his works as God did from his.
Hebrews 4:10

Agentleman once described restless leg syndrome for me. He said, "It feels like you need to stretch your legs all the time, and you never get comfortable. And you can't rest because you keep moving your legs." Thankfully, there's medication for restless legs, but what's the cure for a restless spirit?

The theologian Augustine reveals the source of rest for believers in this beautiful prayer: "Lord, you have formed us for yourself, and our hearts are restless 'til they find rest in you." Abundant rest for our souls is found only in the one who created us. All the rest you're longing for is available to you in Jesus Christ.

Father, help me to be able to quickly discern when I'm spiritually restless, and to hurry to You for rest and refreshment that You provide when I seek You.

MONDAY

Therefore, while the promise of entering his rest still stands, let us fear lest any of you should seem to have failed to reach it.

Hebrews 4:1

Written music contains both notes and rests. Playing the notes is important; but if you miss the rests, the music gets all jumbled! There's one special rest called a fermata. When you come to the fermata, it means you hold on and don't play anymore until the conductor says so. It's not just a rest – it's an intense rest.

God invites you to look to Him as the conductor of your life and to receive the permanent rest that He brings through Jesus Christ. No more wandering about, questioning your purpose, or fearing you can't be right with God. No more fear that pain and difficulty will last forever. God's rest, provided through Jesus Christ, cannot be broken. It is secure now and will last for eternity.

Father, Thank You that the rest that You give me in Your Son, Jesus Christ, is good medicine for my weary soul. Help me to be reminded today, that I don't have to work to earn Your favor.

TUESDAY

*Come to me, all who labor and are heavy
laden, and I will give you rest.*
Matthew 11:28

A missionary translating the Scriptures into a native language couldn't find a word for faith. One day a man
from the village came into his office. He had walked miles,
and when he arrived, he just sort of collapsed wearily into
the chair. The missionary asked, "What's the word for what
you just did?" The man told him, and at that moment, the
missionary had the exact word to express faith to the people.

That's a picture of real saving faith. It's resting all of
who you are on Jesus. Only that kind of rest brings salvation. And once you're saved, it's the kind of rest available to
you day by day as you walk with Jesus Christ.

---

*Lord Jesus, Thank You that I can trust You completely to save
me. Today, help me to enjoy Your rest, knowing that salvation is
Your gift to me, simply for taking You at Your word.*

WEDNESDAY

Sanctify them in the truth; your word is truth.
John 17:17

When stuck in traffic, I look for a traffic report on the radio. I know that the person giving the report has a greater vantage point than me, and He knows the routes to take to avoid the worst traffic. Now, if I was wise, I'd check the traffic report before I get on the road, so I can avoid the mess, instead of trying to find my way out of it.

The Bible is God's traffic report. God sees what we don't see, and He knows what we don't know. His Word penetrates the deep issues of life and provides us the information we need to navigate through life successfully. So, open it up before you meet your problems head on!

Father, I'm thankful for the Bible! I trust that what You say in Your Word is the right path for me to follow, and that it will always lead me in the right direction.

Thursday

Remember the word that I said to you: "A servant is not greater than his master." If they persecuted me, they will also persecute you. If they kept my word, they will also keep yours.

John 15:20

As Americans, we don't know much about persecution. But right now, someone on earth is suffering deeply because they follow Jesus. People are languishing in prison right now for their faith in Christ. Some are being beaten and taken from their families, just because they follow Jesus like you do. They will not forsake following Jesus.

Have you committed your life to Jesus Christ, no matter what? Will you follow Him when it hurts you, or when people don't understand? When your family rejects you? Jesus promises that you will be persecuted if you follow Him. He has also promised to never forsake you when standing for Him is hard. It's worth everything you have, to follow Jesus.

Lord Jesus, You are my master. Help me to never shrink back from following You when it brings hardship. And Lord, help those who are suffering today for the sake of Your name.

Friday

Jesus answered, "O faithless and twisted genera-
tion, how long am I to be with you and bear with
you? Bring your son here."
Luke 9:41

Every beginning swimmer learns early the skill of float-ing on their back. At first, a spotter helps you put your head, arms, and legs just where they need to be. Mostly, they help you stay calm when you think you're sinking! But you soon learn that if you just sort of lay back, the water will hold you up – every time.

Jesus can hold you up in the most difficult circumstanc-es, but you have to trust Him. Maybe right now you're fac-ing something that seems too hard. Instead of being faithless and going the wrong way, trust Jesus. He can use you in powerful ways when you trust Him to hold you up.

Lord, sometimes when life is hard, I feel like I'm drowning. You've
promised that You won't let me drown and that You'll never leave
me. Lord, hold me up today and grow my trust in You.

SATURDAY

An argument arose among them as to
which of them was the greatest.
Luke 9:46

In weight training, the best way to build your leg muscles is to do squats. You lay a heavy barbell across your shoulders, and then squat. And the deeper you squat, the stronger your legs become when you stand up. The further down you go, the more you work out your hamstrings. The lower you go, the more strength you develop.

Jesus told His prideful disciples that humility is the pathway to greatness in God's kingdom. How low are you willing to reach to others for the sake of Jesus Christ? Will you serve others in Jesus' name when there's no advantage to be gained? Humility is the only pathway to greatness.

Lord Jesus, help me to be like You, living for the approval of God through humility and obedience. Help me to say no to my natural desire to seek greatness among men.

Sunday

You make known to me the path of life;
in your presence there is fullness of joy; at your
right hand are pleasures forevermore.
Psalm 16:11

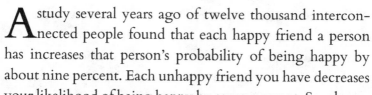

A study several years ago of twelve thousand interconnected people found that each happy friend a person has increases that person's probability of being happy by about nine percent. Each unhappy friend you have decreases your likelihood of being happy by seven percent. So, choose your friends well. Hang out with happy people if you want to be happy. Science shows that.

The Bible teaches us something even better: When you are living in a close relationship with Jesus, His joy will become your joy. Jesus' joy is contagious. His joy will increase your joy. So, if you're living a joyless life today, get closer to Jesus. Spend time in His presence, because where Jesus is, there is fullness of joy!

Father, real joy is found in Your presence. Lord, help me to purpose to be with You every day, and so experience the joy You make available to me when I seek You.

MONDAY

*Behold, I have given you authority to tread on
serpents and scorpions, and over all the power of
the enemy, and nothing shall hurt you.*
Luke 10:19

In the nineteenth century, David Livingston made extremely dangerous explorations within the interior of Africa. He sought to open what he called a missionary road to bring Christianity to Africa's unreached people. Someone asked him if he didn't fear that this task was too difficult and too dangerous. He answered, "I am immortal until the will of God for me is accomplished."

Jesus Christ has given you authority over anything that would try to prevent you from completing God's purpose for you. Whether daunting or dangerous, God's will for you cannot be stopped as you serve Him in faith. So be bold! In Christ, you can do anything He asks of you.

Father, Thank You for reminding me that You alone determine my days and that You have a holy purpose for my life. Therefore, I can trust You for today and for my future.

TUESDAY

*Nevertheless, do not rejoice in this, that the spirits
are subject to you, but rejoice that your names
are written in heaven.*
Luke 10:20

Millions of immigrants have entered the United States at Ellis Island. Around seven hundred thousand of those people have paid to have their names inscribed on a wall of honor. As long as that wall stands, those names will be there. That wall won't last forever. When it is gone, the names chiseled there now will be gone with it.

Jesus offers something far better. If you are trusting the blood of Jesus Christ to save you from sin, then your name is written in His book in heaven. It can never be erased. It cannot be destroyed. Your salvation through Jesus Christ is a sure, secure salvation. It will last for eternity.

---

*Lord God, Thank You for the power of the blood of Jesus
Christ that saves me for all of eternity. I praise You for writing
my name in Your book, and that it will be there forever.*

WEDNESDAY

A joyful heart is good medicine, but a crushed spirit dries up the bones. Proverbs 17:22

O nce I visited a large city in central Asia that had once been part of the Soviet Union. I spent most of my time there teaching the Bible to Christian leaders. I also ventured out into the city. I saw that very few people ever smiled. I learned that under communist control, most of them had been brought up to think that smiling and laughing are weak and frivolous. It made for a sad and somber place.

Too many people's lives are emptied of joy. To God, joy is serious business! God wants you to live full of joy. A joyful heart isn't just good for you, but for others around you. So, take your heart medicine: rejoice in the Lord – and smile!

Father, some days it feels as though joy has been completely wrung out of my life. But You've promised to return joy to me when I rejoice in You. Therefore, today, I will rejoice and be glad!

THURSDAY

And he said to him, "You shall love the Lord your God with all your heart and with all your soul and with all your mind. This is the great and first commandment. And a second is like it: You shall love your neighbor as yourself."
Matthew 22:37–39

On the show *House Hunters*, couples who want to buy a home are shown three different houses. They carefully consider the inside features, like the layout and the countertops. They compare the outside features. They like the pool on this one, but the landscaping's better on that one. But they never, ever examine the neighbors! A house may be great, but having difficult neighbors is challenging.

What kind of neighbor are you to the folks on your street, at work, at the gas station, or at the grocery store? Jesus said that a good neighbor does good for a person in need – even someone drastically different from you. Being a good neighbor in Jesus's name brings Him glory.

———————

Father, I need Your grace to be a good neighbor today – on my street, at work, or at the grocery store. Help me to love You first, so that I can love my neighbors like You do.

Friday

For the whole law is fulfilled in one word:
"You shall love your neighbor as yourself."
Galatians 5:14

Have you ever looked down into your gas tank to see if you've got enough fuel? Of course not, because you can't see down into the tank. But you can look at the fuel gauge. It keeps you informed about your fuel level.

God has given you a gauge of your love for Him, and that's your love for others. It's impossible to really love God if you don't love those made in His image. Real love for God will outflow in love for your neighbor, especially those who are hard to love.

Father, You've commanded me to love people that I sometimes don't even like! Lord, I need Your grace today to love others as I love myself. Even more, help me to love them like You love me.

SATURDAY

But he, desiring to justify himself, said to Jesus,
"And who is my neighbor?"
Luke 10:29

Jimmy sat alone at the dinner table, staring at a plateful of green peas. His mother said, "You're not leaving this table, Jimmy, until you've eaten your peas." He looked at his mom and asked, "Which ones do you want me to eat?"

The Lord says, "Love your neighbor." Sometimes we ask back, "Which ones, Lord?" Well, that's not the way it works! Loving your neighbor means loving whoever comes across your path, even when they're different from you. When they don't share your opinions or your values. When they're not lovely or loveable. When you feel unable to love your neighbor, Jesus will love them through you if you ask Him.

Father, help me not to live deciding who I will love
and who I won't. Give me a heart like Yours, Jesus,
that loves every person.

SUNDAY

And behold, a lawyer stood up to put him to the test,
saying, "Teacher, what shall I do to inherit eternal life?"
Luke 10:25

The headline of an article read, "World Death Rate Holding Steady at One Hundred Percent". Then it said, "Officials say that death has long been our top health concern. It is responsible for one hundred percent of all recorded fatalities. Despite ongoing efforts from the medical community, there is no cure."

That was written tongue in cheek, for laughs. But it highlights this truth: Death comes for all of us. But God has made eternal life possible through His Son, Jesus Christ, who died on the cross to pay for your sin. God raised Him from the dead to give you eternal life. What must you do to inherit eternal life? Only one thing: Surrender your life to Jesus!

Father, thank You that because of Jesus, death is not final for me. You've given me eternal life. Help me to live boldly, knowing death cannot hurt me.

MONDAY

*And Shecaniah the son of Jehiel, of the sons of Elam,
addressed Ezra: "We have broken faith with our God and
have married foreign women from the peoples of the land,
but even now there is hope for Israel in spite of this."*

Ezra 10:2

A submarine sank off the coast of North America in
the Atlantic Ocean. As rescue divers approached the
wreckage, they began to hear tapping noises. As they closed
in, they realized they were hearing a message in Morse
code. A sailor trapped inside was desperately tapping out
the message: "Is there hope? Is there hope?"

Every person is asking that question in the deepest part
of their heart. Without hope there can be no joy, no courage, and no future. The Bible gives us great news: Hope
is alive and it is found in Jesus Christ! If you know Jesus,
you have the greatest hope there is. Hope lives because Jesus
lives! Share that hope with someone today who needs to
know.

---

*Father, there are so many people who are lost and have no hope.
Help me to share Jesus with those around me today who desperately need the hope that Jesus offers.*

45

TUESDAY

And Jesus, looking at him, loved him, and said to him, "You lack one thing: go, sell all that you have and give to the poor, and you will have treasure in heaven; and come, follow me."

Mark 10:21

My friend Dan is a great guy. He served on the church finance team for years. He was on the welcome team every Sunday. Dan was at church all the time. But he said, "I didn't know Jesus. I wasn't saved." I said, "Why were you so active at church?" He said, "I was hiding from Jesus by serving."

Some people hide from Jesus in plain sight by serving at church. Maybe they sing in the choir or teach Sunday School. They might serve as a deacon, or in the parking ministry. But they lack one thing: they've never surrendered their life to Jesus! If you're not saved, don't hide from Jesus Christ any longer. Give your life to Him today.

Lord Jesus, I know that You are God, and that I can never hide from You. I surrender my life to You today. Thank You for giving me treasure in heaven when I give all I am to You.

46

WEDNESDAY

*But the Lord answered her, "Martha, Martha, you
are anxious and troubled about many things."*
Luke 10:41

Novelist Nora Roberts was asked how she balanced work
and family. She said, "It's like juggling. Some of the
balls you're juggling are plastic, and some are glass." She said,
"If you drop a plastic ball, no big deal. It just bounces. You
can pick it back up. But if you drop a glass ball, it shatters."

Martha was so busy the day that Jesus visited her home,
she might have missed time with him completely. The most
precious things in our lives are our relationship with Him,
our fellowship with Him, our knowledge of Him, and our
growth in Him. Other things can be dropped and picked
back up. But if you drop Jesus, you'll miss the most important thing in your life.

---

*Lord Jesus, I admit that many days I'm too busy to give You my
attention. But You are always better than my to-do list. Help me
to say no to my task list long enough to be with You every day.*

THURSDAY

"But one thing is necessary. Mary has chosen the good portion, which will not be taken away from her."
Luke 10:42

Once when I was making dinner for Michele, I put some beautiful ribeye steaks on the grill. They looked so good. Then I went to the kitchen and made some mashed potatoes. I mean they were fluffy and smooth and buttery. But did you know that if you ignore a steak long enough it will literally melt through the grates on the grill? The potatoes could have waited, but the main course required my attention!

When Jesus visited their home, Martha was busy, but Mary was paying attention. Martha was distracted. Mary was devoted. Jesus was gracious to Martha, but He honored Mary's choice and protected it. Don't let your time with Jesus be stolen away by the busyness of the day.

Father, I know that the best thing is to be with You. But my life is busy, and I get so distracted that I don't give You my attention. Lord, I'm sorry. Help me to choose You over busyness.

Friday

*Now Jesus was praying in a certain place, and
when he finished, one of his disciples said to him,
"Lord, teach us to pray, as John taught his disciples."*
Luke 11:1

As a kid, I listened to adults in my church pray. Some of them used fancy words I didn't understand. I learned when I was an adult that some of the words they used, they didn't even understand! They just thought they were good words to use when they were praying.

Prayer is simply talking to God. You don't have to use super-spiritual words or a special formula when you pray. Jesus gave us a pattern for prayer, but He left the specifics to us. Look at Jesus's prayers, Paul's prayers, or Peter's prayers, and you'll see that there are all kinds of ways to pray. So don't be shy; just talk to God today. He loves to hear from you.

---

*Father, Thank You for listening to my prayers when I call out to
You. Thank You for listening to my heart, rather than listening
for impressive words. Help my prayer life to grow as I seek You.*

SATURDAY

Therefore, since we are surrounded by so great a cloud of witnesses, let us also lay aside every weight, and sin which clings so closely, and let us run with endurance the race that is set before us, looking to Jesus, the founder and perfecter of our faith, who for the joy that was set before him endured the cross, despising the shame, and is seated at the right hand of the throne of God.
Hebrews 12:1-2

Police trainee instructors have a secret for testing a trainee's ability to focus. An instructor will unexpectedly put a squeaky rubber chicken up to a cadet's ear. Sometimes the comical prop is dangled just inside the recruit's peripheral vision. It's funny, but the trainee is required to focus despite the distraction and maintain composure. For a police officer, the ability to focus is non-negotiable. It can be a matter of life or death.

Satan dangles distractions in front of us to divert our focus from Jesus Christ. Don't let anything, even a good thing, distract you from Jesus and His desire for your life. Fix your gaze on Jesus; your life depends on it.

Father, help me keep my eyes fixed on Jesus Christ, no matter what this day or season brings. Thank You for His perfect example of ignoring distractions and focusing on the goal!

SUNDAY

*Through him we have also obtained access by faith
into this grace in which we stand, and we rejoice
in hope of the glory of God.*
Romans 5:2

In 2007, Vifill Atlason, a sixteen-year-old from Iceland, decided to call the president of the United States. He somehow obtained the phone number that got him into the innermost workings of the White House communications system. Amazingly, he was connected to the president's personal secretary, who took his contact information. Shortly, Iceland police arrived on Vifill's doorstep. Not just anyone gets access to the president of the United States.

Every born-again follower of Jesus Christ has unrestricted access to the God of the universe through prayer. The broken body and the shed blood of Jesus Christ provides your security clearance to approach Him. So, pray; God will answer.

---

*Father, on my own, I could never come close to You.
But because of Jesus, You welcome me into Your presence.
Thank You for making the way for me to approach You!*

Monday

You desire and do not have, so you murder. You covet and cannot obtain, so you fight and quarrel. You do not have, because you do not ask.

James 4:2

One year, the kids church softball team I played on won the championship. After the final game, my buddy Michael asked the coach if he could have the game ball, and he gave it to him. My mom had taught me not to ask people for things. But here's what I know: every time I visited Michael's house, on the shelf in his room was that game ball, because he had asked for it.

God cares about you! He isn't offended when you ask Him for something you desire. He knows how to say no if that's best. So don't edit your own prayers; let God do the editing. Tell God what you want. Then allow Him to give you His best answer.

———————

Father, forgive me for not always asking You to give me the desires of my heart. It's true that You might say no, but You also might say yes. Help me to ask in faith and leave the results to You.

TUESDAY

Many are the plans in the mind of a man,
but it is the purpose of the LORD that will stand.
Proverbs 19:21

A friend was taking her two grandsons to school. The younger, who was four, said, "Grandma, I'm going to pray, and ask God to turn me into a giraffe." His older brother said, "God won't answer that prayer." His grandmother said, "Oh, God will answer that prayer, and the answer is no!"

No is God's response to some of our prayers. When God tells you no, or wait, it's because He's got something much better for you than what you think you want. God always answers our prayers. Whether He says yes, no, or wait, God is always good, kind, and loving. You can trust His answers to all your prayers to be good and right.

Thank You, Lord, for answering all of my prayers. Help me to learn to wait, to watch, and to listen for Your answers, and help me to be thankful, even when You say no.

WEDNESDAY

But do not overlook this one fact, beloved, that with the Lord one day is as a thousand years, and a thousand years as one day.

2 Peter 3:8

When you approach a railroad crossing, if the lights begin to flash and the bars come down, you know that a train is coming. As the train's engine roars past you, you know only one thing for certain: not how long the train will be, or if there will be a delay, but you can know that the last car will eventually pass. The train could have ten cars or one hundred cars, but the last car on the train will come.

We know that Jesus is coming again. It could be in ten minutes or in a hundred years. The important question is this: Right now, are *you* ready for the return of Jesus Christ? Get ready! Today could be the day.

Lord, should today be the day of Your return, I want to be ready. Help me to be about Your business today, preparing myself and helping others to be prepared for that day.

THURSDAY

But rejoice insofar as you share Christ's sufferings,
that you may also rejoice and be glad when
his glory is revealed.
1 Peter 4:13

A hungry little girl asked her mom for a snack. "How about a raw egg?" asked her mom. "No!" said the girl. "Would you like some flour, or a cup of oil and a little baking soda?" The little girl scrunched up her nose and said, "No, mommy!" "Well," said her mom, "what if I mix those things together and make you a cake?" That was more what the little girl had in mind.

The circumstances of our lives are sometimes distasteful. The heat of our trials can be hard to bear. God uses both the sweet and the bitter ingredients of our lives, and even fiery trials to make us like Jesus Christ. Each ingredient is necessary, and He doesn't waste a thing.

Lord Jesus, Thank You for not shrinking back from the hard things required to save me. Give me grace to accept the bitter things of life so that I can become more like You.

Friday

*Husbands, love your wives, as Christ loved
the church and gave himself up for her.*
Ephesians 5:25

In 1955, Frank Sinatra recorded the hit song, "Love and Marriage." The lyrics say, "Love and marriage go together like a horse and carriage." The thought of a horse and carriage stirs visions of love and romance, unless you envision a scene from an old western where the hitch breaks, the horse gallops away and the carriage goes careening out of control. In other words, if love has left a marriage, then the marriage is headed for the rocks.

God specifically commands husbands to love their wives. Every marriage can use more love. You can ruin a dessert with too much sugar, but you'll never mess up a marriage with too much love.

Father, I desperately need Your grace to love others. I pray for the husbands in families that are close to my heart today. Help them to truly love and care for their wives.

SATURDAY

The heart of man plans his way,
but the Lord establishes his steps.
Proverbs 16:9

Imagine that you're headed from the West Coast to the East Coast of the United States with a specific destination in mind. If you're traveling just one foot from east to west, and you're one degree off, you'll miss your target by 0.2 inches. If you're traveling from San Francisco to Washington DC, and you're off by one degree, then you'll end up on the other side of Baltimore, missing your destination by forty-two miles. Tiny divergences from your route make a significant difference in where you end up.

Adhering to God's Word and His direction is necessary to stay on target in your life. Veering from His truth, even just a tiny bit, will throw you off course. Faithfully obeying God's Word will keep you on the right path.

Lord, Your Word is an infallible guide for every step I must take in my life. Help me not to veer from it, even a tiny bit, so that I stay firmly on the good path that You have for me.

SUNDAY

For you were bought with a price.
So glorify God in your body.
1 Corinthians 6:20

Several years ago, the mechanical rabbit at a greyhound racetrack malfunctioned and burned up during a race. The dogs were suddenly lost. Some chased their tails, some just lay down on the track, panting. One kept running, missed the turn and slammed into a fence, breaking several ribs. Why? Their purpose for running had burned up. Not one dog finished the race.

Many people spend their lives chasing things that will eventually burn up. But we were created to bring God glory! Jesus redeemed us with the price of His own blood so that we could live to please God. When your greatest aim is God's glory, then you'll experience the real purpose for which you were made.

Lord, Thank You for purchasing my life with the blood
of Your Son, Jesus Christ. I belong to You, God.
Use me today to bring You glory.

MONDAY

*Or do you not know that your body is a temple
of the Holy Spirit within you, whom you have
from God? You are not your own.*
1 Corinthians 6:19

My friend's little girl sucked her fingers when she was tired. One day when she was getting sleepy, she put those three fingers in her mouth. Her mom said, "Honey, take your fingers out of your mouth."

She took the fingers out of her mouth and left the room. In a little bit, her mom found her in the middle of her bed with her fingers in her mouth. She thought if she went to another place, she could do what she wanted.

We sometimes treat God like that. We obey Him at church, or in favorable situations, but in other areas we do what we want. Remember, your body is the dwelling place of God's Holy Spirit. Therefore, you should strive to please Him everywhere you go.

---

*Father, my body is Your home, and You are welcome here.
Help me to keep all the rooms of my heart clean, so that You
can do Your good work in and through me.*

TUESDAY

*I appeal to you therefore, brothers, by the mercies of
God, to present your bodies as a living sacrifice, holy
and acceptable to God, which is your spiritual worship.*

Romans 12:1

What's your purpose in life? For many it's to become successful. Christian psychologist Dr. James Dobson says many people get to the top of the ladder of success, only to find that it was leaning against the wrong wall. They're pursuing the things that God never made us to pursue.

The Apostle Paul clearly reminds us of our purpose: to live our lives to glorify God. That includes what we do with our bodies: where we go, what we look at, what we listen to, and who we spend time with. Glorify God in your body; that's the purpose statement for every believer in Jesus Christ. That's how we are successful in honoring God.

---

*Lord God, my aim is to please You. Help me set a guard
around my eyes, my ears, my hands, my feet, and my desires so
that all my life honors You.*

WEDNESDAY

*And those who belong to Christ Jesus have
crucified the flesh with its passions and desires.*
Galatians 5:24

Let's say your best friend hands you the keys of his brand new, beautiful car and says, "I just want you to enjoy my car for a week." Hopefully, you wouldn't treat that car like an old clunker! Instead, you'd park it in places so far from the store that you might as well have walked. Why? Because that car isn't yours; it belongs to someone who you care about.

If you are saved, then all of you belongs to God. The good news is this: God's Holy Spirit lives inside of you to empower you to live your life for His glory. So, remember the Spirit who dwells within you and determine to serve God with your life.

---

*Father, I welcome the Holy Spirit's encouragement and convic-
tion in my life today. Thank You for His power in me moment
by moment to say no to sin and yes to righteousness.*

Thursday

The thief comes only to steal and kill and destroy.
I came that they may have life and have it abundantly.
John 10:10

Most people think of abundance in material terms. A home of their own, two cars in the garage, college for the kids, new clothes, vacations, and a substantial amount of money. You know – the American Dream. However, all of that can disappear in a moment. Many of us have experienced loss of material possessions.

God has promised to supply all our needs. Jesus didn't come to give us abundant stuff; He came to give abundant life! Through Christ, God gives us abundant mercy, abundant provision, abundant kindness, abundant pardon, and abundant peace. Those are the provisions of an abundant life. So today, give thanks to God for *real* life – and that He gives it abundantly!

God, You've poured out blessing after blessing on me. Thank You for Your abundant kindness, peace, forgiveness, provision, and mercy. I praise You for Your generous gifts to me.

FRIDAY

And they sang a new song, saying, "Worthy are you to take the scroll and to open its seals, for you were slain, and by your blood you ransomed people for God from every tribe and language and people and nation."

Revelation 5:9

I try to pay the lowest price for everything I buy. You probably do, too. In fact, you may know right now where to find the very cheapest gasoline in town. That's a great thing. But sometimes we expend more money on the gas it takes to get to the cheapest station than we save at the pump. There's just something about a bargain that appeals to us.

Jesus didn't bargain shop for your life. He paid the very highest price for you – His own blood. And because He paid that price, He deserves to be glorified in your life. Today, and every day, let's live to honor God's Son who purchased us.

Lord Jesus, You ransomed my guilty life with Your own blood. No matter what life brings, I will always have a song to sing of Your goodness and mercy. I give glory to Your name!

SATURDAY

So shall my word be that goes out from my mouth; it shall not return to me empty, but it shall accomplish that which I purpose, and shall succeed in the thing for which I sent it.

Isaiah 55:11

As a 23-year-old pastoring my first church, I felt so inadequate to teach those precious people God's Word. I committed to study the Scriptures and to learn how to apply them. Then I would faithfully give that word to God's people each week. God faithfully gave me what to sow each week, but He also gave me bread to eat. I found that I grew spiritually through my own preaching!

None of us in that congregation grew because I'm a great preacher, but because God's Word is powerful to both prepare us for ministry and to feed us. There is one prescription that will both keep you spiritually healthy and prepare you to serve others: Study and obey God's Word.

Father, Your Word is perfect; it cannot fail. I surrender to the authority of Your Word. Help me not to only read it, not only to study it, but to obey it so I will be changed.

SUNDAY

*Then the LORD said to me, "You have seen well,
for I am watching over my word to perform it."*
Jeremiah 1:12

John had been sent to the grocery store for three things: milk, bread, and bananas. Two hours later, he returned with two kinds of cookies, a bag of potato chips, a jar of peanuts, and a package of hotdogs. Oh – and 2 apples, because he wanted to eat healthy. You know what he didn't have? Milk, bread, and bananas. The bags were full, but John really came home empty handed.

God's Word will never come back to God empty-handed. It has supernatural power to accomplish God's purpose in your life. It has the supernatural power as you obey it to transform your life and accomplish God's purpose in you. The Word of God is always sufficient, and you can fully trust everything it says.

Lord God, I confess that my words are sometimes empty; but Your Word is never empty. It is ever powerful and perfectly reliable. By Your grace, I will trust all You have said in Your Word.

MONDAY

For the word of God is living and active, sharper than any two-edged sword, piercing to the division of soul and of spirit, of joints and of marrow, and discerning the thoughts and intentions of the heart.

Hebrews 4:12

Boys around the country used to covet the job of paperboy. They'd deliver the morning paper, rolled and banded nice and tight. A good paperboy could land your paper squarely on the porch, right by your door. Even a champion paperboy could not make you read the paper. His job was only to deliver it.

The same is true in your life. Don't measure your success in sharing the gospel, teaching a Sunday school class, or exhorting a person in sin, by the response of the listeners. If you've faithfully delivered God's Word, you've succeeded. Be ready to share God's Word with everyone as you have opportunity. The results are up to God; His Word is always successful.

Lord, Your Word alone is powerful to bring life. Nothing I say can improve upon the Gospel. Help me boldly share Your Word the best I can and leave the saving to You.

TUESDAY

But understand this, that in the last days
there will come times of difficulty.
2 Timothy 3:1

When the ocean liner Queen Mary was decommissioned in 1967 after serving for three decades at sea, workers began to repurpose the ship as a museum and hotel. They worked to strip thirty layers of paint from the smokestacks. When the paint was completely stripped, none of the steel was left! They had shape and a form, but there was nothing there.

Difficult times are already here! The only way to stand firm during these days is to keep God's Word as central in our lives. Cling to it and obey it day by day. Make it your foundation for living. The only way to confidently face these perilous times is with the Bible in your hand and heart.

Father, every age has been filled with perilous times. Make me
like Your people who came before me who clung steadfastly to
Your Word, even in great difficulty, and overcame.

WEDNESDAY

*But as for you, continue in what you have
learned and have firmly believed, knowing
from whom you learned it.*
2 Timothy 3:14

The past ten years have seen an explosion in the publication of cookbooks. There are at least two cooking channels on TV, and a plethora of other cooking-themed resources. But people aren't cooking! One lady said she's bought fourteen cookbooks and subscribed to three cooking magazines. But she's cooked only one meal at home in the past four years, and she said "That one didn't come out very well."

There are more Bibles than ever before, but fewer people are reading them! Don't depend on what you've learned you learned yesterday, or last week, or last year. You've got to *continue* in your Bible, day after day after day. Your life will remain untransformed if you stay away from God's Word, but God will powerfully change your life as you continue in His Word.

Lord God, forgive me for the days when I've ignored my Bible. I agree with You that the only way to grow in my faith is to continue in Your Word. Thank You for its power to transform me.

THURSDAY

All Scripture is breathed out by God and profitable for teaching, for reproof, for correction, and for training in righteousness, that the man of God may be complete, equipped for every good work.

2 Timothy 3:16–17

When my Uncle Thurman died, they laid him in the casket holding his Bible, which was opened to the passage above. I asked his wife, my Aunt Brenda, "Why did you have Uncle Thurman buried with that passage open?" She said, "That passage was preached at Thurman's ordination, and when he died, he was preparing to preach on that passage." Uncle Thurman loved God's Word, and he kept it in his hands all the days of his life.

As long as I live, I'm going to keep my Bible in my hand, and put God's Word into my heart. That's the only way I can serve the Lord faithfully and know how to please Him. God's Word is His wonderful gift to us. God's Word is profitable for every area of your life. When you love the Bible and obey it, you cannot fail to please God.

Father, help me not only to know the Bible, but to love my Bible. Thank You for Your holy and perfect Word that not only corrects and trains me, but equips me to serve You.

Friday

Convinced of this, I know that I will remain and continue with you all, for your progress and joy in the faith.

Philippians 1:25

In caves and caverns, beautiful mineral formations rise from the floor and descend from the ceiling. The stalagmites and stalactites grow over hundreds and thousands of years as water drips from above, leaving a tiny deposit of minerals with each drop. Over time, those tiny deposits progressively form something beautiful.

The Bible uses the word *progress* to talk about spiritual growth. We grow as we make steady headway on our lifelong journey. Spiritual growth doesn't happen overnight, but it does happen as we follow Jesus day by day for a lifetime. So, stay in God's Word and pray every day. Jesus is building something beautiful from your life.

Lord Jesus, I want to progress in my spiritual life. When my time with You is cut short, help me to grab moments in Your Word so that I keep moving forward, even a little at a time.

SATURDAY

I have been crucified with Christ. It is no longer I who live, but Christ who lives in me. And the life I now live in the flesh I live by faith in the Son of God, who loved me and gave himself for me.

Galatians 2:20

A Christian professor placed his final exam face-down on each student's desk. When the students turned over the exam, they found their name at the top, and that all the questions had already been answered. Then the professor said to the class: "All of the answers are correct. You receive an A because the creator of the exam has taken it for you. You've just experienced grace."

God saves us by grace - not because we're good enough, and certainly not because we've made a valiant effort to earn salvation! Faith in Jesus Christ makes us right with God. Jesus also empowers us to live a life that pleases God. Therefore, we can say with Paul, "I no longer live, but Christ lives in me."

Father, Your salvation is a gift I could not earn. I can't live the Christian life except by the power of Jesus Christ living in me. Help me to live each moment by faith in Jesus Christ.

SUNDAY

Finally, then, brothers, we ask and urge you in the Lord Jesus, that as you received from us how you ought to walk and to please God, just as you are doing, that you do so more and more.

1 Thessalonians 4:1

Our grandmothers and mothers may have had a haphazard collection of recycled butter containers they used to store every leftover in the kitchen. If grandmother sent you for the butter, it was a good idea to lift the lid and see what was inside the container, because there was always a good chance it was yesterday's pot roast.

Don't be confused by people labeling what's evil as good, and good as evil. Calling pot roast butter won't make you able to spread it on your toast! The Bible clearly teaches how we should walk to please God. If you're morally conflicted, God's Word is a faithful guide. Make the determination to be a God-pleaser, not a world pleaser.

Lord, Your Word is clear about what is good and what is evil. Help me to form my convictions based on Your Word and by Your grace. God help me to stand for Your truth, no matter what the world says.

MONDAY

And have put on the new self, which is being renewed
in knowledge after the image of its creator.
Colossians 3:10

A salesman was eager to sell a man a suit that didn't fit. One sleeve was too short, one side of the suit drooped, and one trouser leg drug the floor. So, the salesman told the man: "Just pull your arm up like this. Then kind of lean your hips in like this. And just extend that leg a bit." Performing the suggested contortions made everything fit, and he bought the suit. A woman watching said. "That man can barely walk!" Her friend said, "Yes, but doesn't his suit fit beautifully!"

A life of sin can never fit a person who is truly saved. God will never bend His righteous standard to make you comfortable in ill-fitting sin. So determine that you will clothe yourself with deeds of righteousness and live according to God's holiness. That is the only comfortable fit for a follower of Jesus Christ.

Father, Thank You that Your Holy Spirit makes me uncom-
fortable when my sinful deeds don't fit my new self. Help me to
intentionally put on holy behavior that fits my saved life.

Tuesday

I must perform my vows to you, O God;
I will render thank offerings to you.
Psalm 56:12

Sometimes we pray what people have called *foxhole prayers.* Like a soldier under heavy fire with no way out, we pray, "God, I'm in trouble! If you'll deliver me from this, I will ..." Then we finish our prayer with a promise to God. There's nothing wrong with a foxhole prayer, unless you fail to keep your promise after God answers.

David said that the promises He made to God when he was under duress were binding! Maybe God has graciously answered a foxhole prayer in your life. Whether it was yesterday, or even if it was years ago, keep your promise to serve God with your life. He hasn't forgotten your promise, and neither should you.

———————

Father, forgive me for the empty promises I've made to You.
Help me from this day forward to fulfill my vows to You.
Thank You that none of Your promises are empty. You keep
them all.

WEDNESDAY

In God I have put my trust; I will not be afraid.
What can man do to me?

Psalm 56:11

A man knew that the neighborhood children were terribly afraid of his dog, who sounded vicious. One day he called out, "Kids, you don't need to be afraid of my dog! Look!" The man pulled back the dog's lip to reveal the dog had no teeth – not even one! He said, "If he comes after you, the worst he can do is gum you. He can't really hurt you."

When Jesus Christ died on the cross, He defeated our greatest enemies, death, hell, and Satan. You don't need to fear death. You don't need to fear hell. And you don't need to fear the devil! He may come after you, but he has no teeth!

Lord Jesus, Thank You that You have soundly defeated my enemies. They shake at the mention of Your name. Because You live in me, I don't have to shake before them. Help me not to fear!

Thursday

That according to the riches of his glory he may grant you to be strengthened with power through his Spirit in your inner being.

Ephesians 3:16

I like superhero stories. Usually, the thing that saves their lives as humans also creates their superpower. For instance, the device that protects Tony Stark from dying after surviving a huge explosion, powers his Iron Man suit. So the thing that saved Tony Stark's life also gives him super strength to be Iron Man.

The same Holy Spirit who brings you salvation also provides His power to accomplish what God asks of you. The Holy Spirit helps you overcome temptation and to endure in trials. The Holy Spirit helps you to deal with difficult people and to have joy in impossible circumstances. He gives you power to do what you could never do on your own. Simply ask in prayer, and God will supply all the power you need.

God, I am powerless to do anything courageous or good, except that You live in me and work through me. Father, fill me with Your Holy Spirit right now and empower me to live for You.

FRIDAY

Rejoice in hope, be patient in tribulation,
be constant in prayer.
Romans 12:12

Ten-year-old Emmy needed help with arithmetic. She'd heard that her new neighbor, Albert, was good at arithmetic. So, she went and asked him for help. He gladly helped her with her homework.

When Emmy's mother learned what she was doing, she hurried to apologize to Albert for Emmy's intrusion. Albert put her at ease. "I love helping Emmy learn. She's welcome here." Emmy's mom was relieved and said, "Oh, thank you, Mr. Einstein."

Our God is all wise and has all the power in the universe. He longs for you to call on Him in prayer every day with every need. His door is open, and the welcome mat is out. So, bring your entire life to Him in prayer.

God, Thank You for Your open-ended invitation to pray. Help me to pray constantly about everything that concerns me. Thank You that prayer makes me hopeful because You will answer.

SATURDAY

Through him then let us continually offer up a sacrifice of praise to God, that is, the fruit of lips that acknowledge his name.
Hebrews 13:15

On Saturday mornings at our house, my wife Michele is the worship leader. She doesn't usually realize it, but most Saturday mornings as she's doing chores, she begins singing songs that praise God. She sings songs that we love and grew up singing. And when I hear her, I join in. I love the spontaneous worship of our Lord that happens at our house on Saturday.

You ought to find something to praise God for every day. When you praise the Lord, He fills the mundane and even the difficult experiences of your life with joy and worship. Our worship is for the Lord; but it brings a great benefit to our hearts as well! Don't wait for Sunday to worship the Lord. Worship Him continually throughout the week.

God, I praise You! You are the Almighty God, creator of everything, and You are good to all You have made. You are good to me personally! Help me to live each day to worship You.

SUNDAY

Therefore, confess your sins to one another and pray for one another, that you may be healed. The prayer of a righteous person has great power as it is working.
James 5:16

A pastor went to visit sick patients in the hospital. He found all the patients were happy. Each time he entered a room and asked a patient, "How are you today?" the answer was the same: "I'm good!" He asked, "Don't you feel sick? Don't you hurt somewhere?" They'd say, "Nope, I'm as fit as a fiddle! I'm doing really great!" They all needed help; but no one admitted it.

That's a picture of how we often act in church. We come hurting and needy, but we don't want anyone to know. Church isn't a place we go to show everyone that we've got it all together! Church is where we are all in desperate need of God, and of the support and prayers of other believers. Confess your need to other believers and experience the great joy of being prayed for!

Father, Thank You for making me part of Your church. You don't intend for me to live without the love and encouragement of Your children. Give me grace to ask others to pray for me.

MONDAY

And they devoted themselves to the apostles' teaching and the fellowship, to the breaking of bread and the prayers.

Acts 2:42

Years ago, Michele and I traveled to Colorado and for the first time saw aspen trees. We learned that though each of those beautiful trees is individual, underneath they share the same root system. They are nourished together and support one another. They literally cannot survive without one another!

You are certainly an individual, but you are intended to live in community with other believers. We are rooted together in Jesus Christ. God intends that we support one another and nurture one another, and much of that happens in the local church body. So be intentional about fellowship with your church. Make it a point to worship together and to pray for one another. You will grow best when you grow with other believers.

Lord Jesus, Thank You for Your church. Encourage us together as our pastor brings Your Word to us. Grow us toward You and toward one another as we pray and fellowship together.

TUESDAY

*Rejoice always, pray without ceasing, give
thanks in all circumstances; for this is the will
of God in Christ Jesus for you.*
1 Thessalonians 5:16–18

A recent survey reveals what Americans who pray, pray about. Seven percent say they pray for parking spots – and I confess, I'm among that seven percent! Seven percent said they've prayed not to get caught speeding. Thirteen percent pray for their favorite team to win. Lots of people pray. But how should we pray?

Jesus lived His life in constant prayer. He prayed prayers of thanksgiving and praise. He prayed early. He prayed late. Sometimes He prayed all night. Sometimes He prayed before working a miracle. If the one and only Son of God needed to pray, we do even more! So, pray without ceasing.

---

*Father, help me to treat prayer like the air I breathe, knowing
I cannot live without it. Help me to abide in prayer, always
rejoicing and giving thanks, as well as seeking Your help.*

WEDNESDAY

Give us this day our daily bread.
Matthew 6:11

A young girl wrote this letter: "To Whom It May Concern. I'm writing to order three hundred and sixty-five great days. Please deliver them to me promptly." She signed it, turned to her brother, and said this: "I've found out that if you want great days, it's best to order them a year at a time."

Long range planning is great; but long range praying is just about impossible. Jesus instructs us to ask God each day to meet our needs. Like the children of Israel who depended on God's daily provision of manna in the wilderness, God wants us to depend on Him day by day. Ask God to meet the needs you face today. Prayer is trusting God's care, one day at a time.

Lord, You've promised to meet my daily needs, so I'm not going to worry today. I'll trust You today, and I'll trust You again tomorrow. Thank You for Your faithfulness to me.

THURSDAY

And forgive us our debts,
as we also have forgiven our debtors.
Matthew 6:12

O nce I was in a meeting with a friend when another person in the room stood and chewed my friend out. I was very offended by the ugly, unkind things he said to my friend. I remained angry at that guy for a long time. One day as I was praying, the Lord said, "Stephen, have you forgiven that guy?" I admit, I didn't want to forgive him! I enjoyed being angry at him. I sought God's grace, and He made me able to really forgive him.

When we pray, we not only seek God's forgiveness for our sins; we seek God's grace to forgive others who hurt or offend us. Ask God to show you if you are carrying unforgiveness in your heart for someone. God has graciously forgiven us, and so we are to forgive others for His sake.

Father, You've freely forgiven my sins, and You ask me to forgive those who've sinned against me. Give me Your supernatural strength, Father, to forgive them and to let those offenses go.

FRIDAY

*This is the message we have heard from him
and proclaim to you, that God is light and in
him is no darkness at all.*

1 John 1:5

A missionary was shopping for a globe of the world to display in her station. There were two options: One globe was very basic. The second globe was much nicer and had the added feature of a light inside. As the clerk pointed out the features of both globes, he pointed to the lighted globe and said, "This one is nicer, but, of course, the lighted world costs more."

God paid the highest price to bring light to this sinful world when He sent His Son, Jesus Christ, to die on the cross. When Jesus enters your life, He shines His light through you. That light cost God everything He had; let it shine!

Lord Jesus, You are the light of the world, and You live in me. Help me not to try to hide Your light. Jesus, shine Your light through me to dispel darkness in my home and community.

SATURDAY

*He will be great and will be called the Son
of the Most High. And the Lord God will give to
him the throne of his father David.*
Luke 1:32

Years ago, the great novelist H. G. Wells created his list of the ten greatest men of history. He put Jesus at the top of the list. Perhaps he thought he was doing a noble thing by putting Jesus Christ in the number-one spot on his list. The truth is, Jesus doesn't even belong on that list. He's a list all unto Himself. His greatness is far higher than anyone else's greatness.

Jesus Christ was a man – that is true. He is also God! He is the highest in all of the universe, the creator of the universe, and the Lord over all. Everything that God the Father, is, God the Son, Jesus, is. When you look at Jesus, you see God. He is absolutely unique among men.

---

*Lord Jesus, open the eyes of my lost friends and family to see who
You are – not only the greatest man to ever live, but the Son of
God, the Messiah. Help them to worship You as their Savior.*

Sunday

Pray then like this: "Our Father in heaven,
hallowed be Your name."
Matthew 6:9

Aman visiting an electric plant was amazed at how many signs there were warning people about the power of the electricity. Bright yellow signs with bold letters that said, "Do not touch! Danger; High Voltage! Stay away. Keep back." He thought to himself, "The people who work at this plant surely know how powerful the electricity is." And they did. The signs were there so that they would never forget what they were dealing with.

When you pray, don't forget who you're praying to. God is the almighty creator of the universe. He is all powerful, and above all, He is holy. Let's regard our heavenly Father with reverence and awe.

———————

Lord God, You are holy; I am sinful. You are the creator; I am
Your creation. You are good; there's nothing good in me. You are
my friend, but You are first God of all. I will worship You.

Monday

Jesus said to them, "I am the bread of life,
whoever comes to me shall never hunger, and believes
in me shall never thirst."
John 6:35

Black holes in the universe are created when stars die. The terrific gravity of the dying star pulls in and destroys everything near it. Nothing escapes the hole, not even light. It's a hole, but it also has a heaviness inside that we can't even imagine.

The Bible says that sin brings death. It creates an emptiness and a heaviness in our hearts. Nothing can fill that emptiness or relieve the burden of it. But Jesus died on the cross to lift the heavy guilt of our sin. He rose from the dead to replace emptiness with His hope. Come to Him, and He will fill all the hungry and thirsty places in your life.

Father, when I'm hungry, remind me that Jesus is the bread of
life. When I'm thirsty, help me to remember that He is living
water. Only Jesus can satisfy my deepest hunger and thirst.

TUESDAY

On their return the apostles told him all that they had done. And he took them and withdrew apart to a town called Bethsaida.

Luke 9:10

On their wedding day, brides and grooms promise each other, *I take you*. Does that mean, "*From now on I'll take you out to eat every weekend?*" No! *I take you* means, "To have and to hold, from this day forward; to love and cherish, for richer, for poorer; in sickness or health, until death parts us." That's what *I take you* means.

When Jesus saves you, He takes you. You become His to love and cherish. He loves and cares for you no matter your circumstances. No matter your sin. No matter your financial status. No matter your level of strength or ability to perform. Salvation doesn't create a casual relationship with Jesus, but one of depth and intimacy, forever.

———————

Lord Jesus, Thank You for taking me as Your own. Thank You for loving me as a bridegroom loves His bride. Help me cherish You as a bride cherishes her groom.

WEDNESDAY

And he said to them, "Take nothing for your journey, no staff, nor bag, nor bread, nor money."
Luke 9:3

When I travel to preach, or to train pastors, I often forget to pack something I need, like my belt, toothpaste, or an extra pair of socks. No matter what I've forgotten, I remain focused on my mission. God's purpose for me to teach and preach His Word is much more important than if I'm on day two of a pair of socks!

Jesus' purpose for your life should be your primary focus. It's so easy to let the details of our lives become distractions and reasons not to obey. Don't wait until everything is just right to obey Jesus. The mission is always more important than your comfort!

Father, You know the things that distract me – my family; my job; my finances. Help me to love You more than these. Give me Your grace to set my focus squarely on Your purpose for me.

THURSDAY

I rejoice at the coming of Stephanas and Fortunatus and Achaicus, because they have made up for your absence, for they refreshed my spirit as well as yours. Give recognition to such people.
1 Corinthians 16:17–18

Michele and I like to watch baking shows where the contestants make these beautiful show-stopper cakes. Really, the cake is almost inconsequential. They don't talk about the ingredients or how it tastes. The icing is the important thing. It fills in the holes and the gaps and holds everything together. An imperfect cake with the right icing is beautiful, and a whole lot sweeter!

Encouragement is the icing in our relationships. It covers over the imperfections and holds things together. There's somebody in your life who needs your encouragement – maybe even today. So take the opportunity God gives you to encourage that person. They will be refreshed and strengthened when you do.

Lord, give me words of encouragement to share with someone who is beaten down or discouraged today. Help my words be like a drink of cool water to someone who is weary.

FRIDAY

*For a wide door for effective work has opened to me,
and there are many adversaries.*

1 Corinthians 16:9

A shoe salesman saw when he got to his new territory that no one wore shoes. He called the home office. "Send me somewhere else," he said. "Everybody here goes barefoot. I can't sell shoes here" So he left. When the new salesman arrived, he excitedly called the home office, and said, "Send all the shoes you can! Everybody here needs shoes!"

People who oppose the gospel are those who need the gospel the most. If you're living where there's opposition, or if there are few Christians where you are, that's an opportunity for you to share the good news of the gospel of Jesus Christ. God gives us opportunities to spread the gospel; we need to take them.

Father, give me courage to share Jesus where I am. Hold back the adversaries of the Gospel and help me to walk through open doors and share Jesus Christ with the lost.

SATURDAY

The wicked borrows but does not pay back,
but the righteous is generous and gives.
Psalm 37:21

A man climbing a snowy mountain got colder and colder as he gained elevation. He was losing strength and afraid of frostbite. Soon he came upon a stranger, collapsed and unconscious in the snow. The climber sprang into action, wrapping the frozen man in his own coat, and vigorously rubbing his arms and legs to warm him up. As he worked, he warmed up also.

God calls us to be generous. When we give to others, it blesses us as well. Share what you have, even if it is little. Blessings are ours when we take the opportunity to help others.

———————————

Father, You've graciously provided everything I need, not just for myself, but so I can share with others. Show me opportunities to share with others so I can experience Your blessings.

Sunday

*Therefore I tell you, her sins, which are many,
are forgiven—for she loved much. But he who is
forgiven little, loves little.*
Luke 7:47

You know the feeling. You're at the doctor's office, sitting on the examination table. The doctor asks you to cross one leg over the other. Then he takes a little rubber mallet and sharply strikes your leg, right below your knee-cap. When he does that, you don't think about it, and you don't make it happen, but your leg kicks out. It's a reflexive response. You can't help it.

When God lovingly and graciously pours His forgiveness for your sins into your heart, there should be a reflexive response of love for Him. Then the forgiveness you've received from God should encourage your forgiveness and love for others. Take stock of how much you love; it's a measure of how much you've been forgiven.

---

*O God, Thank You for showing mercy to me, a great sinner!
Strengthen me when I'm tempted to withhold mercy from others,
and help me to forgive them as You've forgiven me.*

MONDAY

*Wait for the Lord; be strong, and let your
heart take courage; wait for the Lord!*
Psalm 27:14

I read about a guy who was cooped up with his family on a houseboat for a whole year while it rained cats and dogs. No sun, only clouds, rain, thunder, and lightning for a year! We don't even like being stuck inside from the rain for a week. Waiting is tough, but it's often how we experience God's plan. Just ask Noah.

If you're tired of your present situation, pray, wait faithfully on Him, and don't be discouraged. Experiencing God's best requires patience and obedience. It sounds contradictory, but moving forward with Jesus sometimes means standing still. God is actively working for your good, even while you wait.

———————

Father, I don't like waiting! But I want to be faithful and obedient as I wait. Help me to stand still and stay close to You while You work where I cannot see, all for my good and Your glory.

TUESDAY

Now concerning our brother Apollos, I strongly urged him to visit you with the other brothers, but it was not at all his will to come now. He will come when he has opportunity.

1 Corinthians 16:12

Nicole and her two-year-old son Clark were watching the local high school homecoming parade. Nicole didn't realize when Clark began choking on a piece of candy, because he made no noise. When she saw he had turned blue, Nicole frantically screamed for help. When Tyra, a cheerleader riding on a parade float, heard Nicole's cries, she jumped from the float and ran to help. Tyra saved Clark's life because she was trained, she was ready, and she was willing when she was needed.

Opportunities sometimes arrive disguised as impossible situations. God can use you in mighty ways when you are trained, available, and willing to serve when He sends opportunities your way. So prepare to serve, to teach, to share, and to encourage. You never know when an opportunity will present itself.

Lord, help me to view every impossible situation as a stage to see You work. Help me to be prepared for You to use me when unexpected opportunities arise. I want You to use me.

Wednesday

Be watchful, stand firm in the faith,
act like men, be strong.
1 Corinthians 16:13

When our son Joshua was about seven years old, he played on a church basketball team. His coach wasn't very good. He constantly told the boys, "Focus!" He'd say, "Joshua! Sam! Tyler! Focus! You need to focus!" That's all he said. One day Michele said, "They don't know what to focus on! The coach never tells them. They don't even know where the out of bound lines are!"

If all God said was, *"Stand firm!"* but didn't tell you where to stand, that would only be frustrating. God says, "Stand firm *in the faith*." Don't waver in your belief in the Gospel of Jesus Christ. Don't waver in trusting God and His promises. Guard your confidence in the Word of God. Keep your focus on Jesus. He is the object of your faith, and He will help to keep you in bounds. Therefore, you can stand firm in Him.

Father, I want to stand firm in my faith in Jesus Christ. Help me to have laser-like focus on Jesus by staying in Your Word and prayer. When I begin to waver, keep me strong by Your Spirit.

THURSDAY

It (Love) does not insist on its own way;
it is not irritable or resentful.

1 Corinthians 13:5

A man confessed that when he was irritated or angry, he would explode on his family. "When I feel the pressure building, I just blow up. Then I'm over it and we move on." Then he continued, "At least that's what I used to do, until I realized that's what a nuclear bomb does: It explodes, and then it's over, but it leaves a whole lot of damage behind."

The same happens when we explode on a regular basis with the people that we love. Our angry outbursts may relieve the pressure we feel, but it leaves damage in the hearts of our spouses and children, and even our parents and friends. Love is not irritable. Love protects other people. Love never leaves destruction in its wake. Don't let the bomb of irritability explode upon those you love. It's not worth the price of the harm it causes.

Father, explosions of anger are always hurtful and never helpful.
Lord, help me to set a guard over my mouth when I am angry
so that I don't spew irritable, resentful words on others.

Friday

Now there are varieties of gifts, but the same Spirit.
1 Corinthians 12:4

A couple's large clock had died. The husband found what looked like the same clock at a big department store. However, the wife wanted to return to the expensive store where they had bought the first one. "You'll get a better quality clock there," she insisted. Well, the husband traced both clocks back to their manufacturer, he found that both were made by the same company. Similar clocks, sold in different stores, but the same manufacturer. They had equal value.

Your spiritual gift is never less valuable than someone else's. You may use your gift in a much different location or circumstance, but no matter how or where your gift is used, it is from God. Be intentional and use your gift in the body of Christ, wherever you are. Spiritual gifts are never given for our own glory, but to glorify the Lord Jesus Christ and to build up His church.

God, You have made me a valuable part of Your body. Make me aware of the gifts You've given me to serve others, and show me specific ways to use them in Your church.

SATURDAY

Love bears all things, believes all things, hopes all things, endures all things. Love never ends. As for prophecies, they will pass away; as for tongues, they will cease; as for knowledge, it will pass away.

1 Corinthians 13:7–8

In the army, a soldier is responsible for his assigned post. A good soldier never, ever abandons his post. Not for bad weather, or because it's inconvenient. He doesn't leave when it gets really hard, when there's something else he'd rather do, or people he'd rather be with. A good soldier will not fail to guard his post. He endures in his assignment.

The Bible says that love *endures* all things. In the original language of the Bible, the word *endure* is a military word that refers to a soldier standing at his post. So like a good soldier, love doesn't abandon its post. Real love doesn't stop loving. Love endures *all* things. Love never fails.

Father, Your love never fails me. Help me to love my family and to love Your church with that kind of love. Teach me to bear with others like You bear with me.

Sunday

Love does not insist on its own way;
it is not irritable or resentful.
1 Corinthians 13:5

Toddlers are not known for generosity. A toddler's creed says this:

> If I want it, it's mine.
> If I give it to you, but later I want it back, it's mine.
> If I can take it away from you, I will and it's mine.
> If it's yours, but it looks like mine, it's mine.
> It's mine, and it will always be mine.

Adults look more mature and are much more sophisticated. We still have a tendency to focus on *mine: My stuff, my way.*

That's not what love does. Love is willing to take a back seat to the other person's desires. Love doesn't manipulate or sweet talk its way into what it wants. Love isn't insistent on pleasing oneself. Let's not be adults who look mature but are as self-focused as toddlers. Rather, let's love like Jesus loves, always considerate of the other person.

Lord, life isn't all about me. Forgive me for being selfish and rude. I need Your grace to set aside my demands for satisfaction. Help me to consider what others need and to be kind.

MONDAY

Yet I will rejoice in the LORD;
I will take joy in the God of my salvation.
Habakkuk 3:18

A hospice nurse who comforts patients in their final days has observed that many dying people have this one regret in common: *I wish I hadn't worried so much, or let things get to me so badly. I wish I'd let myself be happier.* There is something much better than happiness. Happiness is dependent upon our circumstances. Your current situation, though it makes you quite happy, can go from wonderful to devastating in moments.

Real joy doesn't fluctuate with your circumstances because the wellspring of joy is Jesus! Joy is found by delighting ourselves in Him and living to please Him. Hard circumstances can't change real joy because they can't change Jesus. If you are depending on circumstances to make you happy, then it's time to shift your focus to Jesus and find joy!

Lord, I love it when joy is easy; but sometimes, joy is a choice I must make. I always have reason for joy because Jesus saved me from my sin. Help me to always choose joy.

TUESDAY

Love is patient and kind; love does not envy or boast; it is not arrogant or rude. It does not insist on its own way; it is not irritable or resentful.

1 Corinthians 13:4–5

A desk clerk at a hotel became a punching bag for people unhappy with their rooms. They were rude and unkind when they complained to him. The clerk noticed that their facial expressions changed dramatically when they were being rude. So, he put up a big mirror behind his desk, where the complainers couldn't help but see their own faces. When unhappy, complaining people saw their reflection in the mirror, they tended to not be as rude. Let's face it: rudeness doesn't look good on anybody.

Love is never arrogant, boastful, or rude. Rude words can ruin your testimony for Jesus. So every day, breathe a prayer and ask God to help you be patient and kind. Love communicates with kindness, even when you're unhappy.

Lord, there are so many arrogant and rude people; I don't want to be one of them. Help me to shine the light of Jesus by loving people with patience, kindness, and humility.

WEDNESDAY

And he called the twelve together and gave them power er and authority over all demons and to cure diseases.

Luke 9:1

Most people feel inadequate in some area of their life. But as many as eighty percent of millennials say, *I'm not good enough* - in virtually every area of their lives. There's bad news: we are all inadequate. We all sin and fall short of God's glory. We'll never measure up.

There's also very good news: Jesus Christ, God's perfect Son, is enough! And the best news is that Jesus is enough for you, personally. Jesus knows all of your weaknesses and shortcomings. He is faithful, and He will strengthen you to do all He asks of you. You can have confidence because Jesus is enough for you, every day.

Father, Thank You that Jesus Christ lives in me and gives me His power and authority to do everything He asks of me. I am insufficient, but in Jesus Christ, I can confidently serve You.

THURSDAY

*Love never ends. As for prophecies, they will
pass away; as for tongues, they will cease;
as for knowledge, it will pass away.*

1 Corinthians 13:8

I confess, math isn't my strong suit. Here's a mathematical truth that I understand clearly: anything times zero is zero. So let's say that on a scale of one to ten, you've got level ten understanding of the Bible and spiritual things, but your love factor is zero. If you multiply your knowledge by your love, you get zero. Or let's say you're the highest giver in your church, but you have zero love. The result? Zero.

Love is the factor that gives value to all of our deeds for Jesus Christ, even if our resources are limited. So give, with love. Serve, with love. Speak, with love. God will multiply whatever resource you bring to Him by the factor of your love to make it more than you ever imagined for His kingdom.

Father, when everything else has passed away, Your love will remain. I'm thankful for Your faithful love. Fill me with Your love to fuel my giving, my serving, and my words.

Friday

And if I have prophetic powers, and understand all mysteries and all knowledge, and if I have all faith, so as to remove mountains, but have not love, I am nothing.
1 Corinthians 13:2

If you've ever done any work with epoxy glue, you know most often, epoxy comes in a syringe with two tubes – one containing resin, which is really thick, gooey, and sticky. The resin looks like it would work on its own. But it won't. It just makes a sticky mess unless you combine it with the activator in the second tube. The activator combined with the resin will work to hold things together. Resin without the activator is nothing.

Great works are nothing without love. Love is like an activator in our lives. When love is the foundation of your life, you can form tight bonds with your spouse and kids, your church, and with your friends. As you serve the Lord and others, make sure to start with love.

Father, You do not measure my life by my impressive deeds, but by my love for You and others. Help me to love You with all that I am and have, and to love my neighbor as myself.

SATURDAY

And he said to them, "Why are you troubled, and why do doubts arise in your hearts?"
Luke 24:38

Michele and I love to travel. Sometimes we plan trips to locations that are east of us. And sometimes we go to locations that are west of us. We've never been able to travel east and west at the same time. If we did, we'd never get anywhere. We'd just be unable to move. Paralyzed.

Doubting God is like trying to go east and west at the same time. It's paralyzing! When you're struggling or hurting, when you don't know what to think, and you've got real unanswered questions, bring your doubts and questions to Jesus. He already knows your doubts; He won't condemn you for your questions.

Father, when I'm tempted to doubt You, Thank You for allowing my honest questions. I trust You to faithfully lead me when the way is hard and I can't see where we're going,

SUNDAY

*But the Pharisees and the lawyers rejected
the purpose of God for themselves.*
Luke 7:30

What if you're out of gas, and when you pull into the filling station they say, "Hey, we're out of gas, but we've got water. You want to fill up with water?" Well, no. "It's really great fizzy, fruit flavored water." No. "It's the best water in the world, from an artesian well in Fiji." No! A gasoline engine cannot fulfill its purpose by any other fuel but gasoline.

C. S. Lewis once said that just as a car is made to run on gas, God designed you to run on Himself. Your life's real purpose cannot be fueled by anything other than God. Embrace God's purpose for your life, which is first of all to become like His Son Jesus Christ. Put the right fuel in the tank by entrusting all of who you are to God. It will take you as far as you need to go.

---

*Father, Thank You for giving my life real purpose. You have
redeemed me for Your glory so that I can enjoy a relationship
with You. Help me to be more like Jesus Christ every day.*

107

Monday

The voice of the LORD makes the deer give birth and strips the forests bare, and in his temple all cry, "Glory!"
Psalm 29:9

There are many words you might use to describe yourself. If you could condense everything about yourself into one word that would tell me all that I need to know about you, what would it be? Can't think of it? Well, I can't think of it for myself either.

God has many attributes. He is holy. He is merciful. He is jealous and will tolerate no rivals. He is faithful and will never desert us. He is eternal. He is incomprehensible; no one can fully understand Him or figure Him out. He is love without end. But the Bible says that we can describe all of who God is with one word: glory! God is indeed glorious. And it is wonderful that He shines His glory not only in His creation, but through His people. Let God display His glory through your life today.

Father, there is no greater purpose for me than to bring You glory. Please fill all of me with all of You today so that Your glory is displayed in my life.

Tuesday

*And said to him, "Are you the one who is to come,
or shall we look for another?"*
Matthew 11:3

Years ago, when I needed a quiet place to study for my
PhD exams, a monastery in my area graciously welcomed me to rent a room there. On the day I arrived, one
of the monks, dressed in long robes, met me outside and
asked me this familiar question: "Are you the one who is to
come, or shall we look for another?"

That's the very question that John the Baptist asked of
Jesus as He suffered in prison for serving the Lord. So when
God allows pain in your life, don't be afraid or shy to bring
God your questions and your doubts. He is not offended by
your honest questions. He won't turn you away.

---

*Lord Jesus, You are my Savior and my God. There is no other
hope for my life. You are good, patient, and kind. Thank You
that I can bring my questions to You when I am hurting.*

WEDNESDAY

But some of them said, "Could not he who opened the eyes of the blind man also have kept this man from dying?"
John 11:37

It would be pretty foolish to step out onto a rotten bridge over a deep gorge, even if you believed with all your heart that it wouldn't fail. But even if your confidence is shaky, you step out onto a new steel-enforced concrete bridge, and it will hold you. Your faith in the bridge doesn't hold you, it's the bridge itself.

The death, burial, and resurrection of Jesus Christ are the rock-solid foundations of our salvation. Your security doesn't depend on how strong your faith is, but on how strong Jesus is. The object of your faith, Jesus Christ, will never be shaken, even when your confidence is shaky.

Lord Jesus, You are my rock. Life is shaky, but You are not. When I go through tough circumstances, You are still faithful and mighty. I am safe as long as I stand on You.

Thursday

But taking her by the hand he called, saying,
"Child, arise." And her spirit returned, and
she got up at once. And he directed that
something should be given her to eat.

Luke 8:54–55

Have you ever been told, "Something's different about you." It's often your hair: it used to be long, now it's short. Or it used to be one color and now it's another color. Maybe it used to be there, and now it's gone! We often experience superficial changes.

Jairus's entire reality was changed when Jesus raised his dead little girl to life. Jesus has amazing power to change our painful circumstances, and sometimes He does that. But even if He doesn't, He can transform your heartbreak and discouragement into joy and confidence in Him. Bring the hard things in your life to Jesus. He wants to change your reality.

Lord Jesus, Thank You for raising me from death to life when You saved me. Life is still sometimes painful, but in You I have hope that brings me joy and peace. Thank You for changing my life.

FRIDAY

Then people went out to see what had happened, and they came to Jesus and found the man from whom the demons had gone, sitting at the feet of Jesus, clothed and in his right mind, and they were afraid.

Luke 8:35

Michele and I once visited a butterfly aviary. We saw each step of the growth of the butterflies. They begin as ugly, fat caterpillars that crawl around, gorging on leaves all day long. But then they stop eating and form a cocoon around themselves. Inside the cocoon, the caterpillar is somehow completely transformed. At the right time, there emerges a beautiful butterfly. It's an amazing process.

None of us are the same person as we were when we came to Jesus. Jesus takes our dirty, sinful lives and wraps us in the cocoon of His cleansing and forgiveness. By His power we emerge as a brand new creation. Jesus radically transforms every life He touches. In Christ, You have a new identity.

Lord Jesus, Thank You for saving me and transforming my life. Help me to spend time with You, learning from You each day how to move forward and grow in the new life You've given me.

SATURDAY

Jesus said to her, "I am the resurrection and the life. Whoever believes in me, though he die, yet shall he live, and everyone who lives and believes in me shall never die. Do you believe this?"

John 11:25–26

A fisherman in the Philippines cast his line from a pier. He yawned really big, and believe it or not, a fish jumped out of the water, into his mouth and down his throat. He suffocated and died! He probably wouldn't have chosen that day, or that way to die.

We really can't choose when or how we die. When you choose to trust in the death and resurrection of Jesus Christ, even if you die, you'll live again. And if the Lord Jesus returns before you die, you'll never die. Physical death isn't the end of life for the believer. Be encouraged by that today!

Lord Jesus, I praise You that You are the resurrection and the life! Even when I lay down my body in death, in You, I will never die. I praise You for eternal life and the hope I have in You.

SUNDAY

*But he answered them, "My mother and my broth-
ers are those who hear the word of God and do it."*
Luke 8:21

A little boy peddled his tricycle furiously down the side-walk. He went once, twice, three times around the block. A curious police officer stopped the boy and asked, "Son, what are you doing?" The boy said, "I'm running away from home." The policeman said, "Okay, but why do you keep riding around this block?" The little boy said, "Because my mom won't let met cross the street."

It's amazing how obedience keeps us close to home, even when we want to run away. Obedience will keep you close to Jesus when you are tempted to go far away from Him. Those who obey Jesus are the true members of His family.

Lord, Your Word points me to Jesus Christ and shows me how to please You. Help me to obey Your Word today and be identi-fied as Your child – a child of the King.

Monday

One day he got into a boat with his disciples, and he said to them, "Let us go across to the other side of the lake."
Luke 8:22

Recently, my wife Michele said, "This world we're living in – I don't like it." The world at large isn't what we hoped for, is it? And sometimes, our disappointments hit much closer to home, affecting our families, or our church. Surprises, sometimes devastating, keep showing up, making the life we'd hoped for the shadow of a dream.

When a peaceful trip across a glassy lake is upended by raging seas, your unfailing hope is to keep following Jesus – to keep listening to Him and to keep obeying Him, even when you feel like you're drowning. Jesus won't let you sink. He will make sure you arrive at the good place He intends for you to be.

Father, Thank You for my security in Jesus Christ. Sometimes You lead me into storms, but You are always with me. Give me grace to trust You and not to fear, because I am safe with You.

TUESDAY

If anyone serves me, he must follow me; and where I am, there will my servant be also. If anyone serves me, the Father will honor him.

John 12:26

Anne Graham Lotz's husband, Denny, is six feet, seven inches tall. She said, "My husband is head and shoulders above everybody, so when I can't see in a crowd how to get where I need to be, all I have to do is hold his hand, stay close, and follow him. He always gets me where I need to go."

Jesus already sees what's ahead for your life. He sees what you can't see and things you don't know. So when you can't see, and when things aren't turning out the way you thought they would, hold His hand, stay close, and follow Him. He'll take you exactly where you need to be.

Lord Jesus, Thank You for leading me. You'll never send me to face the world alone. You are with me, leading me always to the right place at the right time. Help me to stay close to You.

WEDNESDAY

If you love me, you will keep my commandments.
John 14:15

Dog trainer Barbara Woodhouse says that dogs seem to really love their owners. Then she makes this observation: "But true love in dogs is when a door is left open and the dog stays happily within earshot of its owner." If that's the definition of a dog's love, then after thirteen years of having him, our dog Joey didn't love me one bit. If Joey saw an open door, he was gone!

When the door of temptation is open, love for Jesus causes you to say, "I'm staying with you, Lord. I'll listen to your voice, and I'll obey." We will all face opportunities to wander away from the Lord. But continued obedience is the hallmark of those who love Him.

Father, the simple test for knowing if I love You is whether I obey You. Show me where I fail to obey You and help me to repent. Give me grace each day to love You by doing what You say.

THURSDAY

*In the same way let your light shine before others,
so that they may see your good works and give
glory to your Father who is in heaven.*
Matthew 5:16

Michele and I once visited the Louvre in Paris to see the Mona Lisa and other works of art. I well remember the Mona Lisa, but I don't remember the frame at all. Nothing about it stands out in my mind because the frame wasn't meant to be noticed. The frame served only to draw attention to the painting, and the painting gave glory to the one who painted it.

When others see your good works, what they really see is Jesus shining through you. Our lives are simply the frame through which Jesus is displayed so others will see, and then glorify our Father who is in heaven.

Lord Jesus, I want to live today so that You are on full display in my life. Give me grace so that people notice You, not me. I want my life to glorify You.

FRIDAY

"Sanctify them in the truth; your word is truth."
John 17:17

When our son Joshua was about ten, one morning before daylight I noticed his bedroom light was on. I looked in and found him reading his Bible. When I was a seminary professor, a renowned Bible scholar occupied a neighboring office. He always arrived early and stayed late for one reason: to read his Bible.

Whether you're a child or a professor, if you've been saved one year or fifty, God wants you to continually be in His Word. God's Word is the sanctifying power in our lives. We will never outgrow our need for it. The Bible is an endless treasure of the wisdom and knowledge of God. Regardless of your spiritual maturity, God will continue to change your life as you remain in His Word.

Father, Your Word has the power to change my life. Help me to read it and study it every day, so that I can grow spiritually for as long as I live.

SATURDAY

I have stored up your Word in my heart
that I might not sin against you.
Psalm 119:11

Ayoung believer was discouraged about his attempts to read and remember his Bible. He told his pastor, "It's no use. No matter how much I read I always forget what I've just read." His pastor said, "Don't be discouraged. No matter how much water you pour through a filter, you don't collect much, but at least you end up with a clean filter.

Learning God's Word will take a lifetime! Every time you read it, it's cleaning your life. Spend time reading and thinking about God's Word daily. Reading and obeying the Scriptures is the way to live a life that pleases God.

Lord, teach me to love Your Word. I want to learn to filter
all of my life through what You say is good and right.

SUNDAY

"He has filled the hungry with good things."
Luke 1:53

A young single pastor was a pretty good preacher, but he was a terrible cook. He was always embarrassed by his meager contribution of a bag of chips to the church potluck dinners. The ladies in his church would sweetly put his offering right beside the fried chicken and the steaming casseroles. Then they'd hand him a plate and say, "Fill it up, Pastor!" He always arrived with little more than an empty stomach, but they made sure he ate like a king.

We all come to God with nothing. When you're hungry for Him, He will fill you with Himself. He invites you to take as much of Him as you want. When you leave God's table, you'll be satisfied with His goodness and blessings.

Father, Thank You for inviting me to Your table to feast on Your Word. I praise You for filling me with good things that will last forever.

MONDAY

So I am eager to preach the gospel to you.
Romans 1:15

One summer as a teenager I went to band camp. We worked hard learning to play Tchaikovsky's *1812 Overture*. The Boston Pops play that piece almost perfectly every Fourth of July. Tchaikovsky would love it! But if he had heard our band camp rendition of his *1812 Overture*, he might have come and taken every piece of that music back to his grave with him. It was terrible!

Perhaps you struggle when trying to share the gospel of Jesus. You may think you're not very good at it. Jesus loves your faithfulness to share His story, even when you don't do it perfectly. Be faithful to share the gospel the very best you can, because only His gospel is powerful to save everyone who hears and believes.

Lord Jesus, I want to share Your good news. I ask You to make Your message clear to everyone I share with, even when my words aren't perfect.

TUESDAY

My spirit rejoices in God my Savior.
Luke 1:47

Once when I was speaking at a university, I learned that there would be a duet sung by a funeral director, who looked about seven feet tall, and the wife of the school president, who had to stand on tiptoes to reach five feet. By their appearance, I didn't expect very much from this oddly matched pair. In fact, no one looked very excited. Their song was fabulous! They brought down the house.

Mary's heart-song was one of rejoicing in God, her Savior! She made much of God's blessings, not only to her, but to all mankind, in sending His long-awaited Messiah. Don't let your heart-song be something from the top forty! Sing a song of rejoicing from your heart to God for His unspeakable gift of Jesus!

Father, give me a spirit of rejoicing for all You've done for me. I praise You for the gift of Jesus! Sing a song of praise to Him now.

WEDNESDAY

Every way of a man is right in his own eyes,
but the Lord weighs the heart.
Proverbs 21:2

When I was eleven years old, my dad gave me the responsibility of mowing the lawn. I felt really good about my first day in charge – until my dad took me on a tour of the yard to show me where I could do much better. I was responsible for mowing the grass, but I was mowing his grass. I needed to value his lawn the way he did.

When God weighs your heart, if you are saved, then He is weighing a heart that belongs to Him. You are no longer your own; you belong to God. Therefore, carefully guard and take care of what is His by living in holiness and obedience. Order your ways according to God's way, not by what seems right to you.

Lord, my life is Yours because You made me,
and You saved me. Help me to value what You value
and to live according to Your ways every day.

THURSDAY

The LORD searches all hearts and
understands every plan and thought.
1 Chronicles 28:9

I saw an amazing photo on social media from a friend who'd undergone a heart transplant. He added this comment: "Today I held my seventy-one year old heart in my hands." In his cupped hands was his old heart, while his new heart was now working inside his chest. His doctors would now keep a close eye on his new heart to make sure it continues working well.

God thoroughly understands your heart - the thoughts and plans that come from your innermost being. He searches your character, your thoughts, and your motivations. He completely understands your plans. You can hide nothing from God. Carefully guard your heart so that the Lord, who sees, is pleased.

Lord, nothing I think or desire is hidden from You.
Thank You for giving me a brand new heart through Jesus
Christ. Help me to keep my thoughts and plans pleasing to You.

Friday

As far as the east is from the west, so far does
he remove our transgressions from us.
Psalm 103:12

If you travel north to the North Pole and then just keep going, you end up heading south. If you reach the South Pole, and continue on, then you start going north. North and south touch each other at the poles. But you can travel east for the rest of your life and never head west. Same thing with west; you can travel west forever and never reach east. East and west never touch.

God takes our sins as far away from us as the two directions that never touch – east from west. God's forgiveness is perfect and absolute. He gets rid of your sin for good. And where there is no sin, there's no guilt.

Father, it is a relief to know that because Jesus died on the cross,
You've completely removed all my sin and will never bring it up
again. I praise You for removing my guilt forever!

SATURDAY

*So Solomon did what was evil in the sight of the
LORD and did not wholly follow the LORD.*
1 Kings 11:6

There was once a king who was always the smartest guy
in the room. His unmatched wisdom impressed visiting leaders from around the world. He enjoyed magnificent
political strength and wealth beyond measure. He had committed himself to serve God, but he decided to withhold
one area of his life from the Lord. He became an unfaithful
husband. He married seven hundred wives and kept a harem
of three hundred girlfriends. His heart was divided, and he
failed in a thousand ways.

King Solomon failed the Lord, not for a thousand reasons, but for one: his heart was divided. Holding back any
area of your life from obedience to God opens the door to
costly sin and regret. Honor God with every part of your
life, and you'll continue to enjoy His blessing.

---

*Lord, show me right now where I'm holding any part
of my life from You. Help me to obey You in every part
of my life so I can enjoy Your blessings.*

127

Sunday

Nothing is covered up that will not be revealed,
or hidden that will not be known.
Luke 12:2

Imagine you're in an empty theater, and suddenly everyone you've ever known begins filing in. You learn that they've all come to see an unedited movie of your life – every action, word, and thought, from the day of your birth until now. I don't know about you, but if that's me, I'm going to frantically head for the exit.

You think, "Wow, I'm glad that movie doesn't exist." But it does! God has the complete, unedited recording of your life, and when it plays, there's no exit. Your only hope is that the film would be destroyed.

That's why Jesus came. God gave His Son, Jesus Christ to die on the cross to destroy the record of all your sin and shame. That's how much God loves you.

God, I would never be able to bear the shame of my sin and guilt before You. Thank You for the blood of Jesus Christ that cleanses me from every sin – even the secret ones.

Monday

"Your kingdom come, your will be done."
Matthew 6:10

Michele and I once sold a home to a Korean family. One day I dropped by to visit, and every pair of shoes they owned was on a rack outside the front door. Their tradition was to not wear shoes in the house. When Michele and I had lived there, we wore our shoes through every square inch of that house. We were no longer the queen and king there. Now this was their kingdom, so I took off my shoes before going in.

When God saves you, you enter His kingdom. You live under His authority and under His rule. You will often find yourself trying to live by your old rules. That's when God reminds us that we are not king of our lives anymore; He is. When you pray, "God, Your kingdom come," it also means, "Lord, I let my kingdom go."

Lord, by faith I let my kingdom go. You are my king, and I surrender to Your authority. May Your will be done in my life today.

TUESDAY

Your word is a lamp to my feet and a light to my path.
Psalm 119:105

One of the most frustrating things that I experience when I travel is the unexpected layover. On a recent flight, my scheduled thirty-minute layover was stretched to two hours because the control tower in the destination city was down due to weather. But I promise, I'd rather have the layover than for my pilot to fly me into a situation where there's no one to tell him about the things in the air or on the ground that he can't see or know on his own.

The Bible is God's control tower for your life. On your own, you can't see everything that God wants you to see, or know everything you need to know to arrive safely at your destination. The storms of life can never disable God's Word. It is perfect, true, and reliable. So read, study, pray, and live God's Word daily. It is the light for your path in every situation.

Father, Your Word is a precious gift. Thank You for lighting my daily path with Your Word.

WEDNESDAY

At the time for the banquet he sent his servant
to say to those who had been invited,
"Come, for everything is now ready."
Luke 14:17

In a woman's home hangs a year's-old envelope and card, beautifully framed. Impeccably addressed to the woman and her husband, the card reads: *The President of the United States and the First Lady Invite you to a Reception at the White House.* Why keep an old invitation on the wall? Because the sender of the invitation makes it significant.

God invites you into His kingdom! He made all the preparations for you to be saved from your sin when His Son, Jesus Christ, died on the cross in your place and rose from the grave. Now He invites you to receive Jesus by faith as your Savior and Lord so that you can be saved from your sin and receive His gift of eternal life. God's invitation to be saved is still open today. Don't let anything prevent you from saying yes.

Lord, thank You for inviting me to be saved!
Thank You for doing all the work and thank You that
I simply need to accept Your invitation by placing my faith
in Jesus Christ to be included in Your kingdom.

THURSDAY

For we walk by faith, not by sight.
2 Corinthians 5:7

Once Michele and I were driving home to see our family. We drove through one state, then another, then another. When we finally crossed into North Carolina, I said, "Honey, we've done so well on this trip, I'm just going to turn off the engine and coast during this last stretch." Of course, I didn't really say that, and I can imagine the look Michele would have given me if I had!

Yesterday's grace from Jesus is not sufficient for today. We need to walk by faith every day, moment by moment relying on His power for hard and even impossible situations. Don't stop walking with Jesus today because you had a great yesterday. Jesus gives grace for today – every day.

―――――――――

*Father, faith is believing what You've said, even when
I can't see what You're doing. Give me greater faith
to continue serving You when I can't see You.*

Friday

Trust in the LORD with all your heart.
Proverbs 3:5

One day as a young boy, I went outside to ride my bike. It had training wheels that held me up; I never wrecked. But that day I saw my dad removing the training wheels from my bike. I panicked! I said "Dad, I need those training wheels!" And he said, "It's time to take them off, son. You'll never really ride a bike until the training wheels are off."

God will sometimes remove the training wheels from your life, so you'll learn to trust Him. When you encounter difficulties that make you feel off balance in your job, your finances, your health, or your relationships, keep riding, and trust God. He loves you and will stay with you as you learn to trust Him.

Lord, I don't like difficult circumstances that make me feel wobbly! Thank You that You will always stay beside me, keep me securely in Your care, and help my faith to grow.

SATURDAY

*"I have made myself a servant to all,
that I might win more of them."*
1 Corinthians 9:19

In the 1970's, many young people mired in drugs and the sexual revolution came to Jesus Christ. Churches were often unwelcoming to the wild-looking hippie converts. But evangelist Billy Graham took a different approach. He unbuttoned his collar and stopped wearing a necktie all the time. He grew his hair a little longer. He laid aside his conservative traditions for the sake of reaching young people for Jesus.

Jesus graciously welcomes into His kingdom every person who calls on Him. Let's hold loosely our rights and our traditions that are not based on God's Word. Let's be willing to change and to adjust our preferences to welcome people Jesus died to save.

God, Your salvation is for every kind of person - all who call on the name of Jesus Christ. Give me a welcoming heart to people who are different than me who You bring into Your kingdom.

SUNDAY

*As for that in the good soil, they are those who,
hearing the word, hold it fast in an honest and
good heart, and bear fruit with patience.*
Luke 8:15

My friend Dr. Tom Eliff was given this great advice by his dad, who said, "Son, the solution to most of your problems is this: Do it right now." Then he broke it down for him. He said, "Do it. Do it right. Do it right now."

God wants His Word to fall on good soil in your life. A heart with good soil says, "God, when You speak, I will do it. I will do it right. And I will do it right now." What is God showing you from His Word that you need to obey today? When you do it, do it right, do it right now, and your life will bear fruit for Jesus.

———————

*Father, Your Word shows me clearly how to obey You. Help
me to do all that You say quickly. Help me not to delay in my
obedience to You. I want my life to be fruitful for Jesus.*

MONDAY

*Again he appoints a certain day, "Today,"
saying through David so long afterward, in the
words already quoted, "Today, if you hear his
voice, do not harden your hearts."*

Hebrews 4:7

I get excited when people seem to be listening intently in church. But sometimes, what they're really thinking about is the Golf Channel and how they can improve their swing. Some are on the Cooking Channel in their thoughts, thinking about what they'll cook for dinner that night. Some are on the Home Shopping Network, making a mental list of what they need to get for the house. They hear God's Word with their ears, but their hearts are channel surfing.

We're each responsible for how we hear God's Word. Today, whether you're in your quiet time, or in a worship service, let God's Word fall into good soil and take root in your heart. It will transform your life.

Father, I want to hear Your voice. Where the soil of my heart has become hard, help me to plow and prepare it to receive Your Word today.

TUESDAY

A sower went out to sow his seed. And as he sowed,
some fell along the path and was trampled underfoot,
and the birds of the air devoured it.

Luke 8:5

A young farmer spent months plowing, raking, fertilizing and watering his field. Now he was waiting for his crop to spring up. He complained to an old farmer, "I've got the best looking farm in the county, but nothing's coming up." The old farmer rubbed his chin. "What seed did you plant?" The young farmer said, "Seed? I didn't plant any seed." The old farmer said. "Well, that's your problem! Nothing grows if you don't plant seed."

We *must* share the gospel with people around us. Other activities may be good, but the only way for people to be saved is to hear and believe the gospel message. Faithfully scatter the seeds of the gospel; then the crop will grow.

Father, there are many ways I can serve and show Your love to
people in my life. But the only way for them to be saved is to hear
the gospel. Help me to sow the seeds of the gospel faithfully.

137

WEDNESDAY

All Scripture is breathed out by God and profitable for teaching, for reproof, for correction, and for training in righteousness.
2 Timothy 3:16

What do Bach and Beethoven, Robert Frost and Emily Dickenson, Jane Austen and Robert Louis Stephenson have in common? Each one was *inspired*. All produced extraordinary music, poetry, or fiction, but all wrote their own thoughts. As inspired as they were, their greatest works are still the thoughts of men.

When we call the Scriptures inspired, we mean it is breathed out by God. It is a word from God that reveals God perfectly. It is without error because our God cannot breathe out any lie. It is authoritative because it is the word of the sovereign ruler of this universe. It is sufficient, giving us everything that we need for life and godliness. You can trust every word.

Father, Your Word is perfect. It is everything You want me to know about You and how I can live for You. Help me to treasure Your Word. Help me to submit to its authority for everything in life.

Thursday

Now the parable is this: The seed is the Word of God.
Luke 8:11

Most seeds are very small. Think about a tiny tomato seed. In that seed is the power to produce a productive tomato plant. Or think about the power inside an acorn to produce a majestic oak tree. Little seeds are amazingly powerful! When planted in the right environment, they will take root and grow.

The Bible describes God's Word as seed – seed that is powerful to change people's lives forever! It contains the gospel of Jesus Christ, which saves and transforms the life of every person who believes. God has given us good seed to sow. So every day, let's scatter the seed wherever we are. When we sow widely, faithfully, and confidently, in due time a harvest will come.

Father, Your Word is powerful to produce Your fruit in my life. Help me to also scatter Your seed into the lives of others so they can be saved and become fruitful for You.

FRIDAY

Why do you call me "Lord, Lord,"
and not do what I tell you?
Luke 6:46

I recently visited my doctor because of pain in my shoulder. She gave me good advice, which I followed. Now I feel better. But what if at my follow-up appointment, she asks, "Stephen, is your shoulder better? Did you take the medicine and do your exercises?" And I said, "Doc, I know you're a good doctor, but I didn't really want to do what you said. By the way, my shoulder still hurts." She would ask why I even came to her in the first place!

If you call Jesus *Lord,* then you should be living in obedience to Him. Salvation always creates obedience to God's commands. Jesus never saves a life He doesn't change.

Jesus, You are the Lord of all; You are my Lord. Give me grace to obey all that You say today. I want to follow You faithfully all the days of my life.

Saturday

*Blessed are you who are hungry now, for you
shall be satisfied. Blessed are you who weep now,
for you shall laugh.*
Luke 6:21

A ncient Greeks referred to the island of Cypress as
the island of Macarios. Macarios means *blessed*. The
Greeks believed that all you needed for a full life could
be found on Macarios. It was such a beautiful and fruitful
place that they believed you could live a fully satisfied life
if you lived on Macarios.

Jesus said that everything you need for a happy, satisfied life is found in Him. When we simply find our life in
Him, He will keep all His promises to us. Every promise that
He gives us satisfies the deepest part of who we are. So many
people pursue satisfaction and never find it. That's because
real, lasting satisfaction is found only in Jesus.

---

*Lord Jesus, You are so good to me. You offer to fill me, and to
give me joy that earthly things can never give. Help me to look
no further than You to experience a full and fruitful life.*

SUNDAY

When the crowds learned it, they followed him, and he welcomed them and spoke to them of the kingdom of God and cured those who had need of healing.
Luke 9:11

Aman lost his watch in an icehouse. He and his friends searched through the blocks of ice, the sawdust on the floor, and around the items stored there. They finally gave up. A little boy entered the icehouse and shut the door. Shortly, he came out with the watch. When asked how he found it, he said, "I lay down on the floor and was really quiet. Then I heard the watch ticking and found it."

We must be still to hear Jesus! We need to listen carefully and obediently. He wants to speak to you. When your desire to listen to Jesus lines up with His desire to speak, that's when you'll hear Him.

Father, teach me to prioritize the time You give me. Help me to be still, to read Your Word, and to hear You speak. Nothing on my daily schedule is more valuable than being with You.

MONDAY

Oh, taste and see that the Lord is good!
Blessed is the man who takes refuge in him!
Psalm 34:8

B*iba,* a very popular restaurant in Sacramento, California, was owned by Italian chef, Biba Caggiono. Diners loved Biba's food, and they loved Biba! When Biba died, business waned, and the restaurant closed. Soon some of Biba's employees opened their own restaurant. Without consent they prepared Biba's treasured recipes and renamed them. Now they're in a legal battle with the family. You can't just make another's secret recipe your own!

Yet, in God's family, you can do just that! God wants you to use His recipe of showing unconditional, sacrificial, overcoming love to those around you: to your neighbors, to your family, even to your enemies. When we love the way Jesus loves, other people will taste and see that our Lord is good!

Father, flavor my life with Your love. Help people to see Your love in me so they are drawn to Jesus.

TUESDAY

*Anyone who does not love does not
know God, because God is love.*
1 John 4:8

In 2021, Emily Johnson couldn't have needed heart surgery without the Covid-19 vaccine. But demand for the vaccine far exceeded the supply in her area. A young woman named Christy Lewis, who was at high-risk for Covid complications, learned about Emily's plight on the very day Christy was to be vaccinated. Christy contacted Emily. Together, the women visited the clinic, where Christy convinced the workers to vaccinate Emily in her place. Christy's sacrifice enabled Emily to have her surgery. Emily said this: "I cannot believe that she gave up something so coveted to a complete stranger."

God shows that kind of love to us through His Son Jesus Christ. His compassionate, sacrificial love transforms us, and it will transform others – even our enemies - as we allow Jesus to love them through us.

---

*Lord Jesus, there is no greater love than Yours. Fill me with Your
sacrificial love for others, and draw them to Yourself so that their
lives can be transformed as You have transformed mine.*

WEDNESDAY

But I say to you who hear, Love your enemies,
do good to those who hate you.

Luke 6:27

In middle school, I went to basketball camp. Before we started the drills, the coach said, "When you run this drill, don't use the basketball; use the medicine ball." They handed us that heavy, maybe eight-pound ball, and we started throwing it and catching it. It was tough. It wore us out. But after we did drills with the medicine ball, the regular basketball felt like nothing.

Loving your enemies is like working out with a medicine ball. It's hard! But if you'll do the heavy work of loving those who hate, abuse, or mistreat you, you'll be better able to love the people you really want to love – your spouse, kids, friends, and parents. Trust Jesus to help you love your enemies. He'll bless you when you do.

Father, Jesus Christ loved His enemies and did good to those who hated Him. Thank You for His example. I trust You to empower me to love my enemies and to do good to them.

THURSDAY

But love your enemies, and do good, and lend, expecting nothing in return, and your reward will be great, and you will be sons of the Most High, for he is kind to the ungrateful and the evil.

Luke 6:35

Imagine that the most hated man in the country found himself in need of shelter, food, and clothing. Imagine that your own precious family has suffered because of his abuses. Imagine the entire nation has rejected him. Would you take him in? That's exactly what German Pastor Uwe Holmer did in 1989 when his family opened their home to the deposed communist leader of East Germany. Pastor Holmer did good to a wicked man hated by his entire country.

You say, "I could never do that!" It's humanly impossible to love like that. But Jesus doesn't have another kind of love. When it doesn't make sense, and there's no upside, Jesus will love your enemies through you if you're willing to obey Him.

Father, teach me to earnestly pray for my enemies and for those who seek to harm me. Thank You that even if they don't change, praying for them will make me more like Jesus.

146

FRIDAY

*Give, and it will be given to you. Good measure,
pressed down, shaken together, running over,
will be put into your lap. For with the measure
you use it will be measured back to you.*

Luke 6:38

In New Orleans, Michele and I had a favorite po' boy
sandwich shop. Every time we got a fried shrimp po' boy,
we'd unwrap our sandwich, and more fried shrimp fell out
of the sandwich than there was stuffed inside the bread.
There was always extra shrimp, and it was so good!

When we generously forgive and extend mercy to others, God gives generously to us. He fills our basket, shakes
it a little, and then presses it down to make room for extra.
Then He fills it until His blessings run out of our basket and
into our laps! God multiplies His blessings to those who give
mercy - to those who forgive.

---

*Lord, You have shown generous, overflowing mercy to me.
Create in me a heart that wants to extend mercy generously to
others. Thank You for blessing me when I show mercy to others.*

Saturday

Bless those who curse you, pray for those who abuse you.
Luke 6:28

Nicky Cruz was born to wicked, violent parents who constantly abused him. He grew to live a life of deep hatred and violence on the streets of Brooklyn, New York. When a preacher named David Wilkerson showed up talking to Nicky about the love of Jesus, Nicky spat on David and threatened to kill him. But Nicky couldn't resist the love of Jesus that flowed through David. Nicky surrendered his life to Jesus Christ and was transformed.

Since then, Nicky Cruz has shared the love of Jesus Christ around the world, even leading his parents to faith in Jesus Christ. That's the kind of overcoming love Jesus has for you and for your enemies. His love will enable you to love others – even those who hate you.

Father, on my own I cannot love people who abuse me. But Your Holy Spirit empowers me to love my enemies like Jesus does. Help me right now to love and forgive those who hurt me.

SUNDAY

And try to discern what is pleasing to the Lord.
Ephesians 5:10

I once worked for an ad agency where I was asked to promote a tree planting ceremony for Mr. Edwards, a local dry cleaner. I worked hard making phone calls, issuing press releases, and sending invitations. Guess how many people showed up? About ten – mostly employees of Mr. Edwards! I felt I'd failed. But my boss said, "Stephen, see Mr. Edwards? He planted the tree and got his picture made. He gave his speech, and now he's smiling and laughing. Mr. Edwards is pleased; that's all that matters."

Even if others reject or misunderstand you, the goal is to please the Lord! No matter what others think, your life will be a success if you please Him. His opinion is the only one that matters.

Father, Your Word tells me how to please You. Thank You for Your Holy Spirit who empowers me to please You. Help me to have the desire to please You alone in every situation.

MONDAY

Teach me to do your will, for you are my God!
Let your good Spirit lead me on level ground!
Psalm 143:10

A man washed his new aquarium really well before adding the water and the fish. The next morning, one of the fish had died. He washed the tank again, then added the water and the fish. Next morning, another fish was belly-up in the tank. He called a friend who kept fish and said, "What am I doing wrong? I washed the tank twice ..." His friend jumped in and said, "No! Don't do that, because residue from the soap will kill the fish!" What the man thought was helpful was really harmful.

Leaders who use harsh tactics - criticism, condemnation, or constant nagging – only hurt their followers. Jesus always leads with love, compassion and grace. We'll lead others well when we lead like Jesus.

———

Father, transform my leadership skills so that I lead like Jesus, with compassion and grace. Help me to be a blessing to those I lead in my family, at church, and at work.

TUESDAY

Blessed are the people to whom such blessings fall!
Blessed are the people whose God is the LORD!
Psalm144:15

A dad overheard his little boy and his two friends as they began to compare their fathers. The first boy said, "My dad's important. He knows the mayor." The second little boy said, "That's nothing; my dad knows the governor." The father wondered what his little boy would say, because he didn't know any important people. Then his son said, "That's nothing. My dad knows God."

Dad, do you know God? Have you trusted Jesus Christ as your Savior and become God's child? Do you live to obey Him – not perfectly, but faithfully? The very best gift you can give your kids is this: know God, love Him, and teach your kids to love Him, too.

Lord, I want to be a blessing to my family. Help me to live for You as I lead my family so that my spouse and my children will want to follow Jesus. Help my family to know that I love You.

WEDNESDAY

For it was fitting that he, for whom and by whom all things exist, in bringing many sons to glory, should make the founder of their salvation perfect through suffering.
Hebrews 2:10

When working a jigsaw puzzle with Michele, sometimes I try to make a piece that looks right to me fit in an empty space. I'll even push a little harder to try to make it fit. But if I force that piece into the wrong place, the puzzle can't be completed. There's only one piece in that entire puzzle made to fit that space and complete the picture.

The Bible says that it was fitting for God to send His Son to suffer and die in our place. Jesus' death on the cross was the final piece in completing God's perfect plan of salvation. Don't try to force salvation another way; no other piece except the suffering of Jesus on the cross will fit God's plan to save us.

Father, You have accomplished salvation through the suffering of Jesus Christ on the cross. What a terrible price He paid, but what a tremendous gift You have given me. Thank You, Jesus!

Thursday

But we see him who for a little while was made lower than the angels, namely Jesus, crowned with glory and honor because of the suffering of death, so that by the grace of God he might taste death for everyone.

Hebrews 2:9

When Air Florida Flight 90 crashed into the icy Potomac River in 1982, rescuers lowered a rope from a helicopter to save Arland Williams. Five different times the rope came to Arland Williams, and all five times he passed the rope to someone else. The sixth time the rope was lowered, Arland Williams was too weak to hold on. He died that day, sacrificing his own safety to hand hope to someone else.

Jesus knew that the only way to hand eternal hope to you and me was to go to the cross and pay the terrible price for sin. His decision was formed by loving obedience to His Father, and by unshakable love for us. His perfect love and His sacrifice bought our salvation.

Lord Jesus, I will never be able to Thank You enough for dying in my place to save me from my sin. Help me to live each day thankful for Your love that drove You to the cross.

Friday

And such were some of you. But you were washed, you were sanctified, you were justified in the name of the Lord Jesus Christ and by the Spirit of our God.

1 Corinthians 6:11

As a kid I collected hats. Once when I was outside after a hard rain, I saw a hat sticking up out of the mud. I picked up that wet, muddy hat, wiped it off as best I could, and saw that it had a logo I really liked. I took that nasty hat home and my mom helped me clean it up. It became my favorite.

Only a boy would pull a nasty hat out of the mud and put it on his head. Jesus Christ reaches down into the muck of our sin, lifts us out, cleans us up, and makes us His own – not because He really likes us, but because He deeply loves us.

Father, it amazes me that You chose to save me from my sin. Thank You for washing my sin away, for declaring me not guilty, and for continuing to grow me into the image of Jesus Christ.

SATURDAY

*Since therefore the children share in flesh and blood,
he himself likewise partook of the same things,
that through death he might destroy the one who has
the power of death, that is, the devil.*

Hebrews 2:14

In the early 1900's, American playwright Wilson Mizner and boxer Billy Smith entered a bar, looking for a fight. They started beating up all these guys hanging around, until only one huge longshoreman was left standing. Mizner threw punch after punch, but the guy wouldn't fall. Billy Smith shouted: "Stop hitting him! I knocked him out five minutes ago." The unconscious longshoreman was simply wedged between pieces of heavy furniture that kept him upright, but harmless.

Jesus Christ delivered the knock-out blow to Satan on the cross of Calvary. The devil may still be standing, but he's already been beaten. Next time he threatens you, stand firm, and remind him of that.

---

*Father, I praise You that Satan was defeated when Jesus died
on the cross and rose from the dead. Help me to live boldly and
confidently for You today, unafraid of the devil's threats.*

155

Sunday

He will not let your foot be moved;
he who keeps you will not slumber.

Psalm 121:3

My family laughs about all the places that I've fallen asleep. I have fallen asleep at the movies and at the airport. I've been to Broadway musicals where I've paid a lot of money to fall asleep. I'd probably fall asleep in church, except I'm the preacher!

Even when we're wide awake, we can't be watchful enough to fully protect our families. No matter how strong you are, no matter how vigilant you are, no matter what security system you invest in, you will never be able to always surround those you love. But God can. He never sleeps. He is your rock and your refuge, twenty-four-seven. You can trust Him with your family today.

Father, I get so tired, but You are infinitely strong and alert to care for me. When I have no strength, help me to remember that You are faithfully guarding me and those I love.

MONDAY

*May our sons in their youth be like plants
full grown, our daughters like corner pillars cut
for the structure of a palace.*
Psalm 144:12

A man passing the construction site of St. Paul's cathedral met three stone masons. "What are you doing?" he asked. The first said, "I'm laying bricks." The second said, "I'm stirring mortar." The third looked up and answered quite differently: "I'm building a great cathedral!"

Parents and grandparents, what are you doing? You might say, "I'm changing diapers, over and over." Or, "I'm teaching this child to tie her shoes." Or, "I'm driving this child to practice." All are important things. But look up! Teach your child God's Word. Pray for your child, over, and over, and over! Your real task, by God's power and help, is to build your child's life for the glory of God.

Father, Thank You for the privilege of sharing You with my children and grandchildren. Help them to know and to love Jesus. Help me to never give up praying for them.

TUESDAY

And God is able to make all grace abound to you, so that having all sufficiency in all things at all times, you may abound in every good work.

2 Corinthians 9:8

Afew years ago, FedEx produced an ad mimicking the movie, *Cast Away.* In the ad, a FedEx worker who has been stranded on a deserted island for several years after a plane crash over the ocean delivers the one package that remained intact after the crash. He had left it unopened all the years he was stranded on the island. Upon handing the package to the recipient, he says, "I'm curious; what's in it?" She replies, "Oh, not much - just a satellite phone, some seeds, and a water purifier." Everything a castaway would need.

Everything your family needs is available to you in Jesus Christ. When you pray for Him to provide, and then His provision comes, you'll be all the more aware that it is He who has provided.

Lord Jesus, You've promised to give me everything that I need. Thank You for your faithfulness to provide for me and my family. Help me to be aware of Your provisions and to be thankful.

Wednesday

And at the time for the banquet he sent his servant to say to those who had been invited, "Come, for everything is now ready." But they all alike began to make excuses. The first said to him, "I have bought a field, and I must go out and see it. Please have me excused."

Luke 14:17–18

Adad asked his teenage daughter, "Honey, how do you think dads can have better relationships with their kids?" She thought carefully and answered, "I think the problem is that dads just have too many tomorrows." He said, "What do you mean?" She said, "It's always tomorrow. *I'll have time for that tomorrow. I'll play with you tomorrow. We'll talk tomorrow.*" She was right. Too many tomorrows.

Parents, do you know God today? Have you trusted Jesus Christ as your Savior? Today is the day to seek God's face and to call on Him. Don't make excuses! Today is the day to seek the Lord.

Father, You have made everything ready for me to have a relationship with You right now. Help me not to offer excuses; help me to seek You today, and not put off my relationship with You.

159

Thursday

For each tree is known by its own fruit.
For figs are not gathered from thornbushes,
nor are grapes picked from a bramble bush.
Luke 6:44

I recently learned about a fascinating animal – the northwest tree octopus. It swings from tree to tree looking for food. They're almost extinct now, but they're remarkable; remarkable, but fake! That story was part of a kids' game-show called *Real or Fake*. Kids are given two or three "facts" and they have to pick out the one that's fake. Sometimes they believe that something fake is real.

Jesus calls us to be fruit inspectors. A genuinely saved life will produce fruit that shows Jesus at work. In other words, you know an apple tree for sure, because it bears apples. If bad behavior characterizes your life, you should really ask yourself the question, "Have I truly been saved?" Don't be fooled; be sure!

Father, I want to know if I am truly saved. Help me carefully inspect the fruit in my life to see if it is good or bad. Then help me to respond to You in honesty, truly trusting Jesus as my Savior.

FRIDAY

So, every healthy tree bears good fruit,
but the diseased tree bears bad fruit.
Matthew 7:17

M y dad can tell by the leaf of any tree what kind of tree it is. Me? I usually don't have a clue – unless a tree has fruit hanging on it. If oranges are hanging on a tree, it's for sure an orange tree. Oranges are the evidence.

Are you a fruit bearer? Is there evidence in your life that you're saved? If there's no fruit, or if your fruit is bad if continual sin characterizes your life, then Jesus says you aren't saved. But you can be saved today. If you will turn from your sin, and call on the name of Jesus, He will give you a brand new life that will bear fruit for Him.

God, search my heart and show me the evidence of my salvation.
Lord, if there is evidence, Thank You for saving me! If there's
not, I turn to Jesus Christ right now. Lord, save me!

161

SATURDAY

*The good person out of the good treasure of
his heart produces good, and the evil person out
of his evil treasure produces evil, for out of the
abundance of the heart his mouth speaks.*

Luke 6:45

A man casually laced his conversation with his friend
with profanity. As soon as he did, he said, "Man, I'm
sorry I said those things. That's not me." His friend said,
"Well then, who is it?" Good question.

What does your speech say about you? Do you regularly use blasphemous, filthy, or ugly words? Do you lie,
or regularly hurt people with your speech? Jesus says that
what's in your heart will come out of your mouth. When
Jesus saves our souls, He also sanctifies our speech. Our
words don't lie; they reveal who we really are.

---

*Lord, help my words to glorify You. You are right; the words I
say reveal the condition of my heart. Lord, I repent of ugly speech
and I ask that You would make my heart and my mouth clean.*

SUNDAY

And he came to Nazareth, where he had been brought up. And as was his custom, he went to the synagogue on the Sabbath day, and he stood up to read.

Luke 4:16

I have learned that sixty-one percent of adults wear some type of corrective eye lenses – either glasses or contacts. Some are farsighted, some are nearsighted. Many have a stigmatism, so everything is just fuzzy. For those with less than perfect vision, corrective lenses help them to have a 20/20 view of what they need to see.

Jesus Christ is the lens through which God wants us to read and examine His Word. Seeing Scripture through the lens of Jesus reveals God's redemptive purpose, from Genesis all the way to Revelation. Ask Jesus to give you 20/20 spiritual vision as you study His Word. He's the one who makes the things of God clear.

Lord Jesus, help me to read my Bible looking for You. Show me Yourself on every page. Thank You that all of the Bible is Your story, and that Your story has changed my life. I love You, Jesus!

MONDAY

Therefore, let those who suffer according to God's will entrust their souls to a faithful Creator while doing good.

1 Peter 4:19

A little girl sat with her family to photograph their yearly Christmas picture. She wore a beautiful red and white dress. She had a puffy eye, a busted lip, a tooth knocked out, and athletic tape wrapped around her hands. Though she was covered in injuries, the truth was that she had done them to herself. The little girl had a condition that kept her from feeling pain.

Her mother said, "I'd give anything if my daughter could feel pain because pain shows us that something is wrong."

Painful circumstances are often used by God to correct things that need to change in our lives. In those times, pain is a gift so that you can be right with God. Don't despise pain. It is a tool of grace that God uses to help His people grow into Christ-likeness.

Father, by faith I Thank You for the gift of pain that keeps me close to You. I trust You to use the pain that You allow into my life for Your good purpose and that You never waste my suffering.

TUESDAY

Beloved, do not be surprised at the fiery trial when it comes upon you to test you, as though something strange were happening to you.
1 Peter 4:12

When my wife makes cookies, I like to watch all the ingredients go in the bowl. The flour and sugar, the butter and eggs, and the cocoa all look so pristine when they are scooped from the containers. But when she turns on the mixer, everything gets all jumbled up. If I didn't know I'd get delicious cookies from that, I might think something was terribly wrong.

Sometimes we feel like God has put us in the mixing bowl, turned on the mixer, and that He has churned us up and turned us upside down. We wonder what good can come from all that discomfort! God is always doing something good in our lives. Even when we face the hardest trials, we can trust that God is working out His good purpose for us.

Lord, I can't see in advance the good that will come from my trials. I will trust You because You love me and promise to use them all for good in my life. Thank You for being good to me.

WEDNESDAY

*The Spirit of the Lord is upon me, because he has anointed
me to proclaim good news to the poor. He has sent me to
proclaim liberty to the captives and recovering of sight to
the blind, to set at liberty those who are oppressed.*

Luke 4:18

During World War II, five hundred American and British POWS had spent three years in a hellish prison camp. On January 28, 1945, US Army Rangers went behind enemy lines to rescue them. One POW, Burt Bank stared vacantly at the Ranger who told him he could go. He couldn't move. The Ranger said, "Man, don't you want to be free?" The word *free* broke through to Burt. He reached up and took the Ranger's hand and walked out of that camp to freedom.

Sometimes we don't recognize the freedom that is standing right in front of us. God sent His Son Jesus to set us free from the prison of sin. Don't refuse your freedom! Turn to Jesus and be set free.

----

*Father, Thank You for sending the good news of Jesus to me.
Thank You, Jesus, that Your death on the cross has purchased my
freedom from sin and guilt. Save me, Jesus, and make me free!*

Thursday

And beginning with Moses and all the Prophets,
he interpreted to them in all the Scriptures the
things concerning himself.
Luke 24:27

The great artist Claude Monet painted forty different scenes depicting the Waterloo Bridge across the
Thames River. Each painting is different – different tex-
tures, different colors, and different conditions. Each painting is also always the same because that bridge is the primary subject of each of the paintings.

Jesus Christ and God's redemption in His name is the
central theme of the Bible. Throughout the Scriptures, the
settings change, the historical eras change, and the people
change. The supreme subject of all of Scripture is always
Jesus. Ask God to show you Jesus as you read your Bible,
both in the Old and New Testaments. You will find Him
on every page.

Father, the Bible isn't sixty-six books. It's one story with many
chapters that all point to Jesus. Help me to understand and love
the story of Jesus more and more as I study Your Word.

FRIDAY

*For the wages of sin is death, but the gift of God
is eternal life in Jesus Christ our Lord.*
Romans 6:23

The Mile High Rope Bridge in North Carolina spans two hundred feet across an eighty-foot chasm. Since 1952, thousands of people have walked safely across that bridge. Once when we were there, Michele and Joshua walked across. I believed it would hold me up, but I had trouble taking that first step. I didn't trust the bridge. I finally stepped out in faith, and it held me up.

We're saved when we not only say we believe in Jesus, but when we turn from our sin and trust Jesus. If you haven't been saved, turn from your sin and ask Jesus for His gift of eternal life. Place your faith in Him, and He will save you.

---

*Lord Jesus, Thank You for dying on the cross to forgive my
sin. Thank You for rising from the grave to give me eternal life.
Jesus, I trust You to save me. I can't be saved any other way.*

SATURDAY

When he was reviled, he did not revile in return;
when he suffered, he did not threaten, but continued
entrusting himself to him who judges justly.
1 Peter 2:23

When our son Joshua was little, he loved jumping from the stairs. He'd jump from the first step, then the second step, and then the third step. By the time he got to the fourth step, he wanted me there to catch him. Then he'd confidently jump from the fifth, the sixth, and sometimes even the seventh step. Why? Because he trusted his daddy to catch him.

You may have long-grown too big to trust anybody's hands to catch you when you jump. But you can entrust your life into your heavenly Father's strong, faithful hands. Even when circumstances are painful, you can live with confidence and joy every day, because God is always faithful, and God is always good.

God, I believe that You are always good. I want to be like Jesus, trusting You to deliver me from painful circumstances at the right time. Please give me grace to wait patiently for You to act.

SUNDAY

When Jesus had received the sour wine, he said, "It is finished," and he bowed his head and gave up his spirit.
John 19:30

An African man was surrounded by family and friends in his last moments before dying. A friend asked, "Tell me, brother: Do you fear crossing over the river of death?" The dying man said, "Oh no, brother, I do not fear, because my Father owns the property on both sides of the river."

Jesus crossed the river of death for you. He finished the work of salvation on the cross so that you can walk each day, held securely in the Father's hands. You can entrust your life as well as your death to Him. If you know Jesus Christ as your Savior, when you come to cross the river of death, God will carry you safely over.

Father, Thank You that You will give me dying grace when I need it. Thank You that because Jesus died, He can help me when my time comes to die.

MONDAY

And they were astonished at his teaching,
for his word possessed authority.
Luke 4:32

Babe Pinelli was the umpire behind the plate as the more famous Babe, Babe Ruth, came to bat. The first two pitches whizzed past the Great Bambino, who held his bat steady. Babe Pinelli called them both strikes. The third pitch came high and outside. Ruth again held his bat, and Babe Pinelli called, "Strike three! You're out!"

Ruth protested. "Everybody here knows that was a ball!" Pinelli said, "Yeah, but mine's the only opinion that matters. You're out!"

Who's calling balls and strikes in your life? Jesus Christ alone deserves the position of authority in your life. Because He is God's Son, because He is God Himself, He is the spring of all authority. His opinion of your life is the only one that really matters.

_____

Lord Jesus, You are the boss of my life and I surrender to Your authority. Help me not to question You, or to insist on my own way. Your way is right, Your way is best, and Your way is good.

TUESDAY

And you have been filled in him,
who is the head of all rule and authority.
Colossians 2:10

Imagine someone has decorated their home featuring framed quotes from different people. There are memorable quotes from statesmen and presidents, poets and novelists, thinkers and philosophers. And somewhere in the mix is even a quote from Jesus Christ.

Where does the Word of God rank in your life? Do you hold it below your own opinions? Do you give it equal weight with the opinions of others? Or does God's Word occupy its rightful place in your heart and life above everything else? God's Word is without error, sufficient, and authoritative over everything and everyone in the universe. What Jesus says has ultimate authority because He is God.

Father, Your Word is perfect and of infinitely higher worth than the words of mere men. Help me to know and obey Your Word, and each day surrender to its authority in my life.

WEDNESDAY

But Jesus rebuked him, saying, "Be silent and come out of him!" And when the demon had thrown him down in their midst, he came out of him, having done him no harm.

Luke 4:35

I was recently driving on the congested interstate around Dallas. I looked in the rearview mirror, and there was a Texas state trooper. I wasn't doing anything wrong, but for just a moment, I thought, "What if I just hit the pedal and take it up to ninety-five miles an hour?" Well, I didn't follow through with that thought. It would have been costly to defy the authority driving behind me!

Our sin nature wants to defy the authority of Jesus Christ. The good news is that Jesus has power to deliver us from our own defiance when we trust Him. Make the determination to submit today and every day to the authority of Jesus.

Lord Jesus, I surrender to You as my Lord. You have the right to run my life. When I am tempted to go my own way, help me to keep in line with Your desires for my life.

Thursday

*But he said to them, "I must preach the good news
of the kingdom of God to the other towns as well;
for I was sent for this purpose."*
Luke 4:43

In the early 1960s, there was a push for parents to bring their kids to parking lot parties. The treat for each child was a sugar cube. After all, what kid doesn't love sugar? Each sugar cube contained a dose of the polio vaccine. As the children ate the sugar cubes, they ingested the vaccine. The party was fun, but its purpose was to deliver the vaccine to save kids' lives.

Jesus' blessings to us are a delivery system for the gospel. The gospel of Jesus Christ is the only thing that saves. We should always work to meet other people's needs, but remember that the purpose of serving others is so we can share the gospel with them so they can be saved.

———————

*Father, help me not to leave out the gospel as I meet the needs of
other people. As I serve others with my hands and my feet, help
me to also use my mouth to tell the good news of Jesus.*

Friday

Behold, I have given you authority to tread on serpents and scorpions, and over all the power of the enemy, and nothing shall hurt you.

Luke 10:19

General Jonathan Wainwright was a POW in a Japanese prison camp during World War II. Camp guards beat him mercilessly. He was starved. Over time he became nearly despondent.

One day an American officer arrived with this news: "The war is over. We have won." Prison camp guards attempted to continue their abuse. General Wainwright stood to his feet, and firmly said to them: "I'm in command here. I have my orders." The prisoner had received authority over his captors.

Those whom Jesus saves are no longer prisoners of sin. Jesus gives you authority over sin and Satan in His name and by His power. So when Satan comes at you to scare you, stand firm and remind him who's in charge.

Father, I praise You that Satan has no authority over my life because Jesus Christ has defeated him. Thank You for sharing your authority with me so that I can live in victory over my enemies.

SATURDAY

For I am sure that neither death nor life, nor angels nor rulers, nor things present nor things to come, nor powers, nor height nor depth, nor anything else in all creation, will be able to separate us from the love of God in Christ Jesus our Lord.
Romans 8:38–39

On August 16, 1987, Northwest Airlines flight 225 crashed just after takeoff, killing 155 people. Only one person survived: four-year-old Cecilia. News accounts say that when she was rescued, they couldn't believe that she had been on the plane, because she was unharmed and perfectly well.

How could this have happened? Because as the plane was falling, Cecilia's mother unbuckled her own safety belt, got down on her arms and knees and wrapped up Cecilia. She wouldn't let her go.

Nothing could separate that little girl from her mother's love. No tragedy, no disaster, no crash, no death. Magnify that a million times and you'll know the love that Jesus Christ has for you.

Father, I praise You that nothing in this world or in all of creation can separate me from Your love. Make me a conduit of Your love to others who are searching for that kind of security.

Sunday

I give them eternal life, and they will never perish,
and no one will snatch them out of my hand.
John 10:28

When I was a boy in North Carolina, my best friend's dad told us that when he joined the Navy he was first stationed in California. When he arrived there, he did what everyone did back then when they joined the Navy; he got a tattoo. From the moment he got that tattoo, it didn't matter whether he felt good about that tattoo or not. He had a tattoo, and it was not going to change.

If you've been saved, it doesn't matter how you feel or how you act on a particular day. If Jesus Christ has saved you then your salvation is secure. It's irrevocable! And when you understand that your salvation is settled, then you can experience God's peace and rest.

Father, I am so grateful for the security of my salvation. Once
I am saved, I can never be "un-saved." I praise You for Your
continued faithfulness to me that cannot be shaken.

Monday

While he was in one of the cities, there came a man full of leprosy. And when he saw Jesus, he fell on his face and begged him, "Lord, if you will, you can make me clean."

Luke 5:12

Michele and I once had an almost pure white carpet installed in our house. That carpet attracted stains like a magnet. We shampooed most of the stains away. There was one stain that the more we scrubbed, the more it spread. It was coming from something underneath the carpet that our carpet cleaner couldn't reach.

The stain of sin can't be removed by a simple change in behavior on the outside. Sin is an internal problem that requires an internal solution. The only solution is the blood of Jesus Christ. His blood has the power to wash away every sin. No sin is too ugly to be removed by the blood of Jesus.

Father, Thank You for washing me in the blood of Jesus Christ to completely cleanse me from my sins. Thank You that I can daily confess my sins to You and experience Your cleansing.

TUESDAY

But now even more the report about him went abroad, and great crowds gathered to hear him and to be healed of their infirmities.
Luke 5:15

A man named Bill was grief stricken over the sudden loss of his wife. He just didn't know what to do. Less than a week after her funeral, Bill bought himself a brand new pickup truck with all the bells and whistles. There's nothing wrong with getting a truck, but having a new truck couldn't drive away Bill's grief.

External pleasures cannot heal internal pain. Drugs and alcohol, spending sprees, entertainment – nothing external can heal the pain of the heart. Jesus can. No pain is too great for Him to heal. Physical pain, grief, loss, or betrayal – nothing is too big for Jesus. So turn your heart to Jesus. He will heal you – from the inside out.

———————

Father, when my heart is aching, You are my comforter. Nothing in this world can heal my pain, but You can. Thank You that You can heal my heart of the biggest hurts in my life.

WEDNESDAY

Wash me thoroughly from my iniquity,
and cleanse me from my sin!
Psalm 51:2

When I was a kid, my sweet grandmother would ask me to help her with the dishes. I'd wash, and grandmother would dry and put the dishes away. Sometimes she'd hand me back a dish I'd already washed. That meant it wasn't clean. Sometimes I just couldn't see what grandmother saw. So she'd scrub the dish herself until it was clean. Only when grandmother said the dish was clean, was the dish really clean.

You can't do what needs to be done to make yourself clean before God. We can't see all our own sin, and we certainly can't clean it up. Praise God, Jesus can! Only when Jesus makes you clean does God say you're really clean.

Lord, I'm unable to cleanse my own sin. I don't even see all of it.
I need You to examine me and show me where I need cleansing.
Then, wash me clean in the blood of Jesus Christ.

THURSDAY

And when he had finished speaking,
he said to Simon, "Put out into the deep
and let down your nets for a catch."
Luke 5:4

David Hayes took his granddaughter Alisa fishing in the pond behind his house in North Carolina. Five-year-old Alisa was using a Barbie fishing pole. When she had to run inside for a moment, she asked, "Granddaddy, will you watch my line?" As soon as the door slammed behind Alisa, something hit her line. David struggled for 25 minutes to reel in the twenty-one pound catfish with a Barbie fishing pole.

Neither skill nor high-quality equipment made David and Alisa successful that day. It was simply this: They went fishing. When Jesus says to let down your net and fish for men, will you obey? Jesus will bring the catch if you'll just go fishing.

Lord Jesus, Thank You that the Gospel is simple enough that even a child can share it. Give me grace to share the good news of Jesus Christ often, and to trust You with the results.

FRIDAY

Oh that you would rend the heavens and come down,
that the mountains might quake at your presence.
Isaiah 64:1

In May of 2020, after nearly a decade long hiatus, US astronauts blasted into outer space once again. It was so exciting.

As I watched the broadcast of the launch, the commentator said this: "With all the turmoil in the world, it renews my hope to see that rocket going into space." I felt renewed hope, as well. It's tremendous to see what human beings are capable of.

But our greatest hope doesn't come from us reaching up into heaven. Our greatest hope comes from heaven reaching down to us. God came down to us through His Son Jesus. Jesus' perfect life, his death on the cross, and His resurrection from the grave give us an eternal hope that will never ever diminish.

Father, when I could never reach You, You reached down to rescue me from my sin through Jesus Christ. Thank You for Your constant presence in my live through Your Holy Spirit in me.

SATURDAY

For no good tree bears bad fruit,
nor again does a bad tree bear good fruit.
Luke 6:43

Several years ago, Michele, Joshua and I were in Athens, Greece. As we toured the city, we saw the streets were lined with beautiful orange trees. Their branches were heavy with plump oranges. Someone asked our guide, "Why don't people pick those oranges?" He said, "The oranges on these trees are so bitter, that you can't eat them at all." The trees do bear fruit, but the fruit is bad.

Good fruit is the result of true repentance. Fruit like faithfulness, purity, holiness, honesty, and generosity - these are the things that Jesus produces in a truly transformed life. Every day, make sure that your life is bearing fruit. A fruitful life is one Jesus can use.

Father, I want my life to bear good fruit that brings You glory.
Help me abide in You today so that Your fruit grows in my life
and shows that I belong to You.

SUNDAY

And you are Christ's, and Christ is God's.
1 Corinthians 3:23

Many things are on my daily calendar – my quiet and study time, meetings, vacation, lunches with friends, doctor appointments – all kinds of things. There's one thing I have on my calendar every day: every evening my calendar reminds me to check all the door locks at our home. When I remember to check the locks at night, it gives me a sense of security so I can sleep.

In Jesus Christ, we have eternal security! God's salvation isn't a hope-so salvation; it's a know-so salvation! Having assurance that you're saved empowers you to live for Jesus as you've never lived for Him before. If you have turned from your sin and are trusting Jesus to save you, then you can be sure: you belong to Christ.

Lord, the greatest thing about my life is that I belong to You. Through Christ, I am secure in Your hand; I am secure as Your child; and I have the certainty of eternal life. Thank You!

Monday

*By your blood you ransomed people for God from
every tribe and language and people and nation.*
Revelation 5:9

In his lifetime, Jim Harrison has donated a hundred thirty-seven and a half gallons of blood. I don't think there's a bumper sticker for that! Why would he donate such a large amount of blood? Well, Jim's blood contains a very rare antibody used to make a vaccine that prevents severely anemic newborn babies from dying. Jim's blood has helped saved 2.4 million babies.

Multiply that millions of times, and you have the blood of Jesus Christ. His blood isn't just able to heal us from disease; His blood is able to save us from our sin. His blood gives eternal life to everyone who trusts in Him. Jesus is the ultimate blood donor.

---

*Lord Jesus, You didn't hesitate to pay the price of Your blood
to save me from my sin. Thank You for the eternal life You've
given me that was only possible through the shedding of Your
blood.*

Tuesday

*So then you are no longer strangers and aliens,
but you are fellow citizens with the saints and
members of the household of God.*
Ephesians 2:19

A mother and daughter entered a beautiful cathedral on a sunny Sunday morning. The sunlight streamed through the stained-glass windows that beautifully depicted the four gospel authors. "Who are those men?" the girl asked. Her mom said, "Well, this is St. Matthew, that's St. Luke, there's St. Mark, and St. John." The girl said, "What are saints, Mommy?" And before her mother could answer, the little girl's eyes got big and she said, "Oh, I know. Saints are the people who the light shines through."

The Bible says that every follower of Jesus Christ is a saint. It doesn't matter that you're not perfect. Saints are to live as God's treasured possession in this sinful world. As we do that, day by day we become more saintly – more like our Lord Jesus Christ.

---

*Father, Thank You for making me a member of Your family
through Jesus Christ. I praise You that though I am far from perfect,
You shine your light through me to show that I belong to You.*

WEDNESDAY

Blessed is the man who remains steadfast under trial,
for when he has stood the test he will receive the crown
of life, which God has promised to those who love him.
James 1:12

Imagine opening your mailbox and finding a really filthy, nasty envelope inside. Not only is it wet and dirty, but it smells bad. You take it out of the mailbox and carefully cut through all that filth and nastiness to get the letter out. Why? Because you know that inside that envelope is a love letter from someone you love with all your heart, and who loves you with all their heart.

In the same way, God sometimes will send His most loving messages wrapped in difficult, sorrowful, and nasty trials. God commands us in the middle of that horrible trial, to embrace it with joy because every trial we receive is fully filtered through His love and mercy.

Father, You are good, You are kind, and You are trustworthy.
You are greater than any difficulty that comes to me. Thank You
that trials are always accompanied by Your love and mercy.

THURSDAY

He caused the east wind to blow in the heavens,
and by his power he led out the south wind.
Psalm 78:26

One day Michele and I were walking on the beach. A fairly strong wind was at our backs, and we were having a great walk. But when we turned around, we found ourselves with the wind in our faces. Suddenly our walk was much harder.

We can walk through life with God's encouraging wind at our backs as we seek Him and obey all He shows us. But when we go our own way, His wind will be in our faces, making our journey difficult. Don't try to get God to change His direction for you; He won't. You will enjoy His blessing and encouragement when you walk with Him, and not against Him.

Father, Thank You for the encouragement that You
give in Your Word. Help me to walk in the direction
You're going, and not try to go my own way.

FRIDAY

*Then Jesus was led up by the Spirit into the
wilderness to be tempted by the devil.*
Matthew 4:1

A smart knife salesman invited someone to wail away at his knife blade with a hammer. Someone else cut through a thick phone book with it. Finally, a woman used his knife to saw through a metal can. After all that, the knife was still sharp enough to perfectly slice a ripe tomato. Those tests weren't to see *if* the blade could be dulled, but to prove that it couldn't be.

The Holy Spirit didn't lead Jesus into the wilderness to see *if* He would sin. It was to prove that as God's Son, Jesus Christ had complete power over sin. God was showing us that Jesus *would not* sin. Through the Holy Spirit's power in our lives, we have the same power over temptation. We'll often be tempted, but we never have to sin.

---

*Father, help me to appropriate Your power to fight temptation
and live to please You. I will depend on Your Holy Spirit to
help me to flee temptation when it comes.*

SATURDAY

Woe to the world for temptations to sin!
For it is necessary that temptations come,
but woe to the one by whom the temptation comes!
Matthew 18:7

I have a friend who for years was an electric lineman. He climbed poles day after day for years. He had the strongest hands of anyone I've ever known. He'd always sort of test you when he shook your hand. He'd squeeze hard – not enough to crush your hand, but to show his strength. You might squeeze back, but then he'd squeeze a little harder. He always had the more powerful hand.

Temptation strong-arms us. It squeezes us, and it's powerful. Jesus is more powerful. He defeated every temptation when He was pressured by Satan. He can provide that same power to you when you face the pressures that the devil throws your way. Jesus wants you to share His victory over temptation.

———————

Father, I know I will be tempted, but I don't have to sin because You've given me power through Jesus Christ to be victorious over sin. Give me grace to walk in that power today.

Sunday

And he said to his disciples,
"Temptations to sin are sure to come,
but woe to the one through whom they come!"
Luke 17:1

Before beginning a project, construction engineers always test the strength of the concrete they're going to use. The concrete is mixed according to specifications, then it's poured into cylinders to harden. Then they put the hardened concrete under tremendous pressure. The concrete can only be used if it doesn't crumble or crack.

Jesus never cracked under the tremendous pressure of temptation. Your circumstances will be different. The essence of temptation – the desires of your flesh, the desires of your eyes, and the pride of life – never change. Therefore, Jesus can identify with every temptation you face. He will give you all the strength you need so that you can stand up under temptation and be victorious.

Father, Thank You that Jesus knows what my temptation feels like, so that He can help me to fight it and win. Help me today to stand strong against temptation, so that I am useful to You.

MONDAY

Being strengthened with all power, according to his glorious might, for all endurance and patience with joy.

Colossians 1:11

In a royal palace in Tehran, Iran, hangs a breathtaking mirrored mosaic. Original plans for the palace called for large mirrors from France to be placed in the entrance way. Those mirrors were shattered in transit. Rather than trashing them, they broke the shards into even smaller pieces. Then they glued the thousands of tiny mirrors to form a brilliant mosaic that is unbelievably beautiful.

All of our lives have been shattered by our sin. But because Jesus Christ bore the full brunt of our sin when He died on the cross, God puts us back together beautifully. He not only forgives our sin but strengthens us according to His glorious might to defeat sin in our lives. You can be victorious over sin because of the power of Jesus Christ.

Father, You strengthen me not just with some power, but with all power so that I can endure temptation, develop patience, and have joy. Thank You for Your power to defeat temptation.

TUESDAY

But whoever drinks of the water that I
will give him will never be thirsty again.
The water that I will give him will become in
him a spring of water welling up to eternal life."
John 4:14

Imagine I'm very thirsty and ask you for a drink of water. Now imagine, that after I drink it you say to me, "Ok, give me the water back." Well, that would be impossible! The water in that glass would now be part of me. It would go into the cells in my body, causing my heart to work better, my brain to work better, and my muscles to work better. That water inside me would change every part of me. It would be impossible to give it back.

God's gift of everlasting life is like the gift of water to a thirsty person. You can't take it back because it's a gift that comes into you and changes you! Praise the Lord today that no one can take your salvation from you.

———————————

Father, Thank You for the security of Your salvation! I am
grateful for Your gift of eternal life that will never diminish and
will satisfy my deepest thirst forever.

WEDNESDAY

*Jesus answered her, "If you knew the gift
of God, and who it is that is saying to you,
'Give me a drink,' you would have asked him,
and he would have given you living water."*
John 4:10

What if I said to you, "I'd like to give you this gift."
Then I extended the gift to you, and you received it.
After that, that gift is yours. Even if I don't like what you're
doing, I can't take the gift back. If I tried to reclaim it from
you, then I would never have really given it to you to begin
with. True gifts are given freely with no strings attached.

Because of our sin, the only thing we've earned or that
we deserve from God is death. God, through His Son Jesus
Christ freely offers us the most wonderful gift: His gift of
eternal life. You must simply accept it. You can't earn it; and
you can't un-earn it. Once received, God will never take it
from you.

*Father, the gift of eternal life through Jesus Christ is secure.
No one can take it from me, and I can't lose it! Thank You for
this precious gift that You give freely to all who ask.*

Thursday

The Pharisee, standing by himself, prayed thus: "God, I thank you that I am not like other men, extortioners, unjust, adulterers, or even like this tax collector."
Luke 18:11

Carrie's family lived next to a chicken farm. One day Carrie complained, "Those chicken houses are the stinkin'est things in the whole world. How can they stand to live so close to anything that stinks that bad?" Her husband responded, "Hon, you do remember that we're hog farmers, right?"

Don't think that you are righteous because you're not as bad as someone else. We're all sinners in need of Jesus! God rejects those who depend on their own righteousness. But He lovingly receives every sinner who humbly confesses their need for God's mercy and trusts Jesus Christ to save them.

God, be merciful to me, a sinner! Thank you that Jesus purchased my forgiveness on the cross so that I can be clean before you.

Friday

For we do not have a high priest who is unable to sympathize with our weaknesses, but one who in every respect has been tempted as we are, yet without sin.

Hebrews 4:15

Boxer Rocky Marciano finished his career undefeated. He knocked out forty-three opponents, but six challengers went toe to toe with him for all twelve rounds. Who do you think knew more about what it was like to fight Rocky Marciano – the boxer who got knocked out, or the one who fought every round, and was still standing at the end of the fight?

Jesus stood against Satan round after round, yet never sinned. So when you face temptation, Jesus understands because He's been there. And because He can identify with your temptation, He's able to give you the victory over that sin, and He's ready to forgive you and give you grace when you fall.

Father, Jesus faced the pressures of temptation like me, but He was victorious every time. Thank You that He sympathizes with me when I am weak, and for helping me to defeat temptation.

SATURDAY

*And she had a sister called Mary, who sat at the
Lord's feet and listened to his teaching. But Martha
was distracted with much serving. And she went up to
him and said, "Lord, do you not care that my sister
has left me to serve alone? Tell her then to help me."*

Luke 10:39–40

O nce at my annual physical, I asked the doctor for a
hearing test. He tested my hearing, then he said, "Stephen, your hearing's fine. Why did you ask me to check
it?" I said, "Well, my wife has asked if my hearing's okay,
because I'm just missing things she says." He said, "You're
hearing well; maybe your listening's not as good."

People came to hear Jesus teach and preach. Many people didn't really listen. We must listen and apply what Jesus
says to our lives. Don't let preaching, teaching, or reading
your Bible reach your eyes and ears but not your heart.

---

*Father, I want to be like Mary, listening to Jesus, but I am so of-
ten distracted like Martha. Help me to not only give You a minute
here and there, but to take time to really listen to what You say.*

SUNDAY

*And this is his commandment, that we believe
in the name of his Son Jesus Christ and love one
another, just as he has commanded us.*
1 John 3:23

My friend Alan was a missionary in China. Once he went to a very remote village where he met an old man who had lived there his entire life. After they had talked for a while, Alan asked, "What do you think of Jesus Christ?" The man looked at him, and said, "Jesus Christ? What kind of a thing is that?"

More than two billion people in the world today have never even heard the name of Jesus. Jesus has sent us to the entire world with His name and His gospel. Every person in the world desperately needs to know the only name that saves: Jesus. Ask God today how you can be part of His mission to help people know Jesus.

Father, there are people all around me who do not know Jesus Christ. Help me to live on mission within my sphere of influence. Father, make me willing to take the gospel everywhere I go.

MONDAY

But the angel said to him, "Do not be afraid, Zechariah, for your prayer has been heard, and your wife Elizabeth will bear you a son, and you shall call his name John."
Luke 1:13

As a young pastor, I often visited a lady named Isabell. She was in her eighties. Isabel always prayed for our church and for my family. She said, "Stephen, age is a funny thing. I used to say I was young. Then I stopped saying I was young, but that I was *younger.* Later I said, *I'm getting older.* Then I stopped saying that, and just said, *I'm older.* Now, I just say, *I'm old.*" Even when she was old, Isabel still prayed.

Elizabeth and Zechariah had prayed for a child for a long, long time. God heard and answered in a surprising and miraculous way that blessed the entire nation of Israel. Never give up praying; God hears, and He answers – in His best time.

Father, You always hear my prayers. You haven't forgotten prayers I've prayed for years. Father, until You answer no, I will keep praying. I trust You to answer at the right time.

TUESDAY

Therefore the Lord himself will give you a sign.
Behold, the virgin shall conceive and bear a son,
and shall call his name Immanuel.

Isaiah 7:14

I remember when we brought our son Joshua home as a baby. Instantly we realized that everything changed! Our priorities; our schedule; our plans – even parts of our personalities changed! Our home was different. Just as a song says: A baby really does change everything.

Author E. T. Sullivan said this: "The greatest forces in the world are not earthquakes and thunderbolts. The greatest forces in the world are babies." Isaiah prophesied that a virgin would conceive and bear a baby boy who would grow up and die for the sins of the world. The life, death, and resurrection of this baby, Jesus Christ, would change us from lost to found, from darkness to light, and from death to life. And He will change you if you surrender your life to Him.

Father, the birth of Your Son, Jesus Christ changed the whole world, and I'm so grateful that it has changed me! Thank You that You loved the world so much that You gave Jesus to save us.

WEDNESDAY

*Blessed be the Lord God of Israel, for he
has visited and redeemed his people.*

Luke 1:68

In seventh grade, I lost my baseball glove at school. Now, I admit that was no great loss to the baseball world. I was convinced my glove had been stolen. So, I went to the vice principal, and he assured me no one had stolen my glove. Then he walked me to the lost and found, and there it was. I reclaimed my glove.

I reclaimed my glove, but I didn't redeem my glove because redemption always requires a price. God redeemed us by paying the full debt of our sin with the blood of Jesus Christ, shed upon the cross. When you trust Christ, you no longer owe the debt of your sin. It has been paid; you've been redeemed.

---

*Father, Thank You that when I was broken and lost in my sin,
You redeemed me with the blood of Jesus Christ. I am grateful
that Jesus paid the high price to make me Your child.*

THURSDAY

For if you live according to the flesh you
will die, but if by the Spirit you put to death
the deeds of the body, you will live.

Romans 8:13

Michele and I once visited the Pacific shore in Southern California. We sat on the beach and watched incredible surfers ride the biggest waves we'd ever seen. It was thrilling to see. Sometimes even the best surfers would wipe out. None of them had enough strength to defeat the crash of those massive waves on their own.

Even as believers, our best strength is still weakness. God's Holy Spirit provides perfect strength that is so much better than our own. When we live by our own power, we will fall. When we live daily in the power of the Holy Spirit, He will keep you from wiping out spiritually.

Father, I don't have the strength to faithfully follow Jesus Christ
on my own. Thank You for the power of Your Holy Spirit that
helps me stand against the things that bigger than me.

FRIDAY

So Satan went out from the presence of the
LORD and struck Job with loathsome sores from
the sole of his foot to the crown of his head.
Job 2:7

Once when I stopped at a chicken restaurant for lunch, I ordered two pieces of fried chicken. "We don't have any fried chicken," said the girl at the counter. I said, "Then, I'd like two pieces of rotisserie chicken." She said, "We don't have any rotisserie." I asked for three chicken strips. Same thing. They must not have expected anybody to come for lunch that day.

The Bible says that followers of Jesus should expect trials. They are a normal part of the Christian life. Suffering is most often not the result of sin in your life; God will show you clearly if it is. So be patient and trust God. He will be faithful to bring you safely through your trial.

Father, help me to be watchful, and give me grace to be
faithful when I face tests. I want to develop stronger faith
and proven character, so that I glorify You in my trials.

SATURDAY

*So that you may not be sluggish, but imitators of those
who through faith and patience inherit the promises.*

Hebrews 6:12

A great thing to do with a child is to help her plant a packet of seeds in a flowerpot, water them, and set them in a sunny window, with the seed packet placed by the pot. It may seem like a long, long time, but when the flowers finally poke through the soil and bloom, they will match the picture on the seed packet. They will have kept their promise.

The Bible is like God's seed packet of promises. In the soil of His providence and time, God's promises bloom. Not all of God's promises are instant, but they are all certain. So be patient; God will keep every promise He has made in His Word.

---

*Father, forgive me for being impatient. Give me grace
to wait patiently for You, not giving up hope, confident that
You will keep every promise.*

Sunday

Therefore, since we have been justified by faith, we have peace with God through our Lord Jesus Christ.
Romans 5:1

In Papua New Guinea, two tribes had been engaged in a blood-feud for generations. The chief of one of the tribes was so motivated to end the feud that he called a meeting with the chief of the enemy tribe. At that meeting, he placed his own infant son in the arms of the rival chief to live with his tribe for the rest of his life. As long as the child lived, hostilities ceased. They called that son *the peace child.*

Jesus Christ is God's peace child. His blood shed on the cross makes peace between us and God. Because He rose from the grave and lives forever, the peace He gives doesn't just last for one child's lifetime; it lasts for eternity.

———————

Father, I have no greater treasure than peace with You. Thank You for making peace with me through the death of Your Son, Jesus Christ, so that I no longer fear You, but can love You.

MONDAY

Jesus said to him, "I am the way, and the truth, and the life. No one comes to the Father except through me."
John 14:6

Y ou've probably heard someone refer to drawing a line in the sand. That means a decision has to be made. You either step across the line, or you stay where you are; you must decide. Once that line in the sand has been drawn, it's impossible to stay neutral.

Jesus Christ is God's line in the sand. It's impossible to remain neutral about Jesus. God doesn't give us the option of believing that Jesus is a good teacher, a great man, or a great example, but then reject Him as the Lord of your life. To be saved, you must step over the line and receive Jesus as Savior and Lord. Jesus is the only way to God; will you cross the line and stand with Jesus Christ?

God, I choose to stand with Jesus Christ. I believe that He is Your Son and the only way to You. Give me grace to be faithful to Him today and all the days of my life

TUESDAY

For where two or three are gathered in
my name, there am I among them.
Matthew 18:20

A little girl quizzed her mom on the way to church, "Mommy, will Jesus really be at church with us today?" "Yes, honey," said her mom. "You mean He'll be right in the room with us, and He'll see what we're doing?" Her mommy said, "Yes, we can't see Him, but He'll be there, hearing and seeing us." The little girl considered this. "Mommy," she said, "Will you please comb my hair?"

Rest assured, Jesus isn't concerned about your outward appearance. He's concerned about whether your heart is clean and prepared for worship. Ask God to show you any place where you're not right with Him. Confess your sin, then, worship God with a clean heart.

Father, You know me so much better than I know myself. Search
my heart right now and show me my sin. Thank You for the
blood of Jesus that cleanses me of sin so I can be right with You.

WEDNESDAY

*I have been crucified with Christ. It is no longer I who
live, but Christ who lives in me. And the life I now
live in the flesh I live by faith in the Son of God, who
loved me and gave himself for me.*

Galatians 2:20

I've got some work gloves in my garage. At first, they were
stiff and uncomfortable. I had a hard time even bending
my fingers in them so I could work. See, those gloves were
not yet surrendered to my hands. But as I've worked with
them, over time, they've become supple and conformed to
the contours of my hand.

In the same way, Jesus wants to wear you like a glove,
filling you with Himself so He can do His work through
you. Surrendering to His purpose for you may feel uncomfortable at times. Your heart may be stiff at first. But eventually you'll become more supple. He will empower you to
become everything He has saved you to be.

---

*Father, Thank You for molding and conforming me to the image
of Jesus Christ so that You can use me. Help me to be a willing
vessel for You to fill for Your service.*

Thursday

*And he went down with them and came to
Nazareth and was submissive to them. And his
mother treasured up all these things in her heart.*
Luke 2:51

In 1982 a lanky shortstop stepped onto the field for the Baltimore Orioles. He didn't get much attention that day. But two thousand six hundred thirty-two consecutive games later, he was known as baseball's iron man. Cal Ripken, Jr. didn't reach his full potential by great talent, but by faithfulness.

Reaching your greatest potential doesn't come through talent, brilliance, personality, or wealth. You reach your potential when you live with iron man faithfulness to God. When you simply say, "Jesus, I will do all You ask," and then depend on His strength as you obey, you will become all that God wants you to be.

Lord, help me to develop the same heart of obedience that Jesus had. Thank You that Your only requirement of me is to be faithful; You will supply all the power necessary for me to serve You.

Friday

And Jesus increased in wisdom and in
stature and in favor with God and man.
Luke 2:52

I recently saw a gentleman wearing a t-shirt that said this: Growing old is unavoidable but growing up is optional. That sounds really good if you're talking about keeping a spry mindset. But it's not good if you don't grow out of youthful foolishness.

Even Jesus grew in wisdom. He became wise, in great part, by being submissive to the God-ordained authorities in His life. Beginning with His earthly parents, Mary and Joseph, God's Son lived a life of obedience. To become wise, we must be submissive like Jesus. Wisdom only flourishes in a submissive heart.

Father, Your Word imparts wisdom to my life. Help me to develop a heart of submission and obedience so that Your wisdom achieves its good work in my life.

SATURDAY

Humble yourselves, therefore, under the mighty hand of God so that at the proper time he may exalt you.

1 Peter 5:6

A grown son lived with his old father. One night, the father asked his son several times to stoke the fire. Each time, the son refused. The dad said, "Son, if you won't help me, I need you to leave." The son became angry and left. After a time, the son came to his senses and went home, sorrowful for his sin. His father gladly welcomed him home. They went to sit down, and the father said this, "Son, before you sit down, please stoke the fire."

If you've been traveling without Jesus, you'll always find Him right where you left Him: at the point of submission and obedience before Him.

God, You have the right of authority in my life. I want a heart that obeys You gladly. Help me to repent of my sin quickly and obey all that You tell me.

Sunday

And do you seek great things for yourself? Seek them not, for behold, I am bringing disaster upon all flesh, declares the LORD. But I will give you your life as a prize of war in all places to which you may go.

Jeremiah 45:5

One day, the great conductor Arturo Toscanini was conducting Beethoven's Ninth Symphony. The audience was absolutely overwhelmed at the beauty and power of the music. When the music ended, the audience jumped to their feet, cheering loudly. They clapped and clapped and clapped. Toscanini bowed and directed the orchestra to stand. Overcome, Toscanini turned to his orchestra and whispered hoarsely, but forcefully, "Gentlemen! We are nothing; Beethoven is everything; everything!"

We are nothing; Jesus is everything! We reach our fullest potential when we stop trying to be something on our own and surrender to His purpose. Then Jesus will work in you so that you can become all He has made you and redeemed you to be and to do.

Father, only You deserve honor and glory and praise. Help me to live for Your glory, and not for my own. When people look at my life, help them to only see how great You are.

MONDAY

And he said to them, "You are those who justify yourselves before men, but God knows your hearts. For what is exalted among men is an abomination in the sight of God."

Luke 16:15

We know how the world measures greatness: by attractiveness, by intelligence, by strength, and by wealth. Somebody said it's beauty, brains, brawn, and bucks. If you have some of those, or a lot of those, the world will say you're great. "He's handsome; he's great." "She's brilliant; she's great." "They're athletic; they're great." "Their business is successful; they're great."

God isn't impressed by these things. Perhaps you have little of what the world values. When you're surrendered to Jesus Christ, and live to serve Him and others, you'll maximize your potential in God's eyes. His opinion of you is the only one that matters.

Father, anything good in me is because of You. You are great; I am not. So take all I am and use me for Your glory. I love You and I want to serve You with my life.

TUESDAY

And he sat down and called the twelve.
And he said to them, "If anyone would be first,
he must be last of all and servant of all."
Mark 9:35

Do you ever feel unappreciated? I heard about an insurance adjuster who sometimes travels hundreds of miles away from home and family to help people who have endured great loss. Sometimes the people he goes to help don't really appreciate it. At times they're unkind, impatient, and demanding. But he goes anyway because he really wants to serve.

The test of whether you're a real servant comes when somebody treats you like a servant. Serving is easier when people are patting you on the back and telling you what a wonderful job you're doing. But when you show up and nobody seems to care, or when your sacrifice seems unappreciated, a true servant says, "I serve you because I serve Jesus."

Father, help me to be a servant who cares for the needs of others
before my own. Help me not to serve with the goal of being
recognized, but with the goal of glorifying Jesus Christ.

WEDNESDAY

So whether we are at home or away,
we make it our aim to please him.

2 Corinthians 5:9

I have a friend who heads a large company that serves four thousand clients. Every year, he takes his fifteen top executives on a golf outing. While they play, they talk about their current challenges, and plans for the future. When they reach the ninth hole, my friend gathers everyone around and says this: "All of our clients have different expectations. Would you rather try to work for all four thousand of them, or for me?" He's simply communicating that they really have one person to please, and that's him.

We really have only one person to please, and that's Jesus Christ. If everyone else is pleased with you, but God isn't pleased, you've failed. If God is pleased, that's really all that matters.

God, I want to please You with my life. Help my love for You
to grow and become the driving motivation to please You.

Thursday

The Lord is good to those who wait for him,
to the soul that seeks him.

Lamentations 3:25

A man asked God, "How much is a million dollars to you?" The Lord said, "It's like a penny." Then he said, "God, how long is a million years to you?" God said, "It's like a minute." The man said, "God, can I have a penny?" The Lord answered, "In a minute."

Sometimes when we're anxious for God to answer our prayers, He asks us to wait. Waiting can be so frustrating! When we have a need, we want God to answer us quickly. Remember, God doesn't operate on our timetable. God's timing in our lives is perfect, and He is always good. God is honored when we wait patiently on Him.

Lord, You have always been good to me. Help me to learn patience as I wait for You. I will continue to seek You, because I trust You to always be good to me.

Friday

Therefore the LORD waits to be gracious to you, and therefore he exalts himself to show mercy to you. For the LORD is a God of justice; blessed are all those who wait for him.

Isaiah 30:18

Once I was in a situation where I needed God to answer my prayer specifically and quickly. I prayed, "God, I need You to do this, and I need it by …", and I gave Him a date. Well, God didn't answer that prayer by the deadline I gave Him, but He did forgive me for being presumptuous! He also reminded me that He doesn't work on my schedule.

We should pray specific prayers. However, it's crucial to be patient and wait for the Lord as you seek His will. Don't try to get ahead of God. Be patient and wait on Him. He will answer, and give you all you need – in His perfect timing.

———————————

Lord, You are gracious and merciful to me. Help me to trust Your perfect timing and to wait patiently for You to meet my needs. You are faithful and will answer at the right time.

217

Saturday

Behold, God is my salvation; I will trust, and will
not be afraid; for the Lord God *is my strength*
and my song, and he has become my salvation.
Isaiah 12:2

The great Christian writer, Oswald Chambers wrote this: "God plants His saints in the most useless places. We say, 'I shouldn't be here because I'm so useful.' God puts His people where they will glorify Him; we are not capable of judging where that is." Chambers' statement is the perfect depiction of the popular phrase, *Bloom where you're planted.*

God doesn't necessarily plant us where we think we'll be most useful. He doesn't always do what seems right to us. He often surprises us. Remember, God is God; we are not. We're not capable of knowing where we'll best glorify God. If God calls you to something, then trust and obey, regardless of how it seems to you.

God, Thank You for putting me in the very best place for me to serve You. Teach me to walk daily in Your strength and to have Your joy as I do what You ask. I will trust You and not be afraid.

SUNDAY

*On his robe and on his thigh he has a name
written, King of kings and Lord of lords.*
Revelation 19:16

In 1941, Nazi forces invaded Athens, Greece. They had taken over the entire city, and at the highest point in the region, they hung their Nazi flag. Late one night, two young boys managed to safely sneak past Nazi guards and remove that flag of oppression. The next morning when people all across Athens looked out, they saw the flag was no longer flying. The people of Athens had hope in their hearts for the future.

When Jesus Christ rules your life, He removes the enemy flag of sin and death and raises His banner of forgiveness and grace. Satan rules by oppression, but King Jesus rules by grace and freedom.

Lord Jesus, I am thankful that You've removed the banner of sin over my life and claimed me for Your own. Help me to walk in Your hope, peace, and grace. You are my King.

Monday

My sheep hear my voice, and I
know them, and they follow me.
John 10:27

One summer in high school, I helped my dad build a garage on our property. We poured the foundation, then put up the walls. Eventually came the time for the shingles to go on the roof. I had never been on a roof before. I was scared to death – not of the height, but of hitting the ground if I fell! Dad knew I was afraid. He said, "Son, you can go back down. If I need something, you can hand it up to me." That day fear kept me from fully serving my dad.

Sometimes fear keeps us from fully serving Jesus. Jesus is strong enough to save you, and He's certainly strong enough to protect you when you serve Him. Don't be afraid; He won't let you fall when you are obedient to Him.

————————

Lord Jesus, You are my Shepherd. Help me to remember that You always care perfectly for Your sheep, so I can follow Your voice without fear. When I become afraid, help me to trust in You.

TUESDAY

*And we know that for those who love God
all things work together for good, for those
who are called according to his purpose.*

Romans 8:28

I love chocolate cake. But have you ever tasted cocoa before it's mixed with the butter and the sugar? It's very bitter! I'm pretty sure that if I had been coaxed into eating a spoonful of cocoa before I'd ever eaten chocolate cake, I would never have been convinced that chocolate cake was wonderful.

We will often experience things that are bitter and hard to swallow. We wonder, "Why is God allowing this tough time in my life?" But God mixes the bitter things in our lives with the sweetness of His presence, His grace and His blessings. The result is always good. Even when you face the hardest trials, you can trust that God is working out His good purpose for you.

---

*God, when bitter circumstances come my way, I will trust You.
I love You, Lord, and by Your grace I will still serve You and
wait patiently for the good that You have promised.*

Wednesday

As it is written in the book of the words of Isaiah the prophet, "The voice of one crying in the wilderness: 'Prepare the way of the Lord, make his paths straight.'"
Luke 3:4

About ten minutes before the end of day, workers in a machine shop stopped work and went to change out of their dirty clothes. One day, everyone looked ready to go, except George. He was still working and dirty. Somebody said, "Hey George! You're not ready!" George smiled and said, "Yes I am." When the whistle blew, George unzipped his dirty coveralls, and underneath he had on clean clothes. George said, "I stay ready, so I don't have to get ready."

Have you prepared the way of the Lord in your life? You get ready by trusting Jesus as your Savior. Then, as a believer, you can stay ready by living each day for Him. So be ready; Jesus could come today!

Lord, help me to keep my heart prepared to meet You by living a holy life and seeking You every day. By Your grace, help me to be prepared for Your arrival, even today!

Thursday

Bear fruits in keeping with repentance. And do not begin to say to yourselves, "We have Abraham as our father." For I tell you, God is able from these stones to raise up children for Abraham.

Luke 3:8

In 2009, in a game between the New York Knicks and the New Jersey Nets, Knicks point guard Nate Robinson took an inbound pass. With a half second to go, he turned to shoot the ball. He swished the basket from thirty feet. It was a beautiful shot – right into the opponent's goal! Nate Robinson needed a change of plan; he was going the wrong way.

Spiritually, if you're shooting at the wrong goal, you need a change of plan. You need to repent. Repentance isn't just being sorry; it's being sorry enough to change. True repentance always bears the fruit of transformed attitudes, words, and actions. Only a life that bears fruit for Jesus is a genuinely changed life.

Lord Jesus, examine my life today. Where I am aiming at the wrong goals, or where I veered from Your way, I repent. Help me to be fruitful for You and to bring You glory.

223

Friday

If any of you lacks wisdom, let him ask God,
who gives generously to all without reproach,
and it will be given to him.

James 1:5

My first puzzle as a kid had just four pieces: a banana, an apple, some grapes and an orange. And each piece had its place on the board. Now Michele and I work harder puzzles – sometimes one thousand pieces or more. We always finish them, but some are pretty difficult.

Life is a puzzle with millions of pieces. None of us can put it together on our own. We may get the edges right, and a section here and there. You and I will never be smart enough, or talented enough, or strong enough to put all the pieces of our lives together the right way. God promises to give us all the wisdom we need. When we simply ask Him for wisdom, He'll answer "yes" every time.

God, please give me Your wisdom in my relationships and in the choices I must make. Thank You that You are generous with Your wisdom. I trust You to give me all the wisdom I need.

Saturday

*Get wisdom; get insight; do not forget, and do
not turn away from the words of my mouth.*
Proverbs 4:5

Christmas may seem like a long time ago today. Think
back. Did you get what you wanted for Christmas?
Some of us got what we thought we wanted but didn't want
it after we got it. Some of us got what we wanted, and now
it's in a drawer somewhere not being used or enjoyed.

Whatever else we might get, the thing we need to get
most is wisdom. God doesn't say for us to get money, education, success, or prominence. God tells us to *get* wisdom;
that requires action on our part! The Bible says that the fear
of God is just the *beginning* of wisdom, so stay in His Word
and in prayer. Ask Him for wisdom. That's where you'll
find all the wisdom you need.

---

*Lord God, Your wisdom is abundantly available in Your Word.
Help me to dig every day in Your Word for the treasures of
Your wisdom and live by it so that I can live without regret.*

SUNDAY

Take my instruction instead of silver,
and knowledge rather than choice gold.
Proverbs 8:10

A man named Neal was slowed by developmental challenges. Sometimes people enjoyed playing pranks on him. "Here's a dime and a nickel," they'd say. "Take whichever one you want!" Neal always took the bigger coin, the nickel. Someone took Neal aside one day and said, "Neal, take the dime! It's worth more." "Yeah," Neal said, "but if I stop taking the nickels, they'll stop giving me money!"

The Bible says that if you've got the choice between great wealth and God's wisdom, take the wisdom. It's the most valuable thing that God can give you. You need God's wisdom to know how to put the pieces of your life in the right place. If you have God's wisdom, you'll be truly rich.

God, Your wisdom is so much greater than wealth. Living by Your principles gives me peace and helps me avoid regret. Help me to choose Your wisdom and not the wisdom the world offers.

MONDAY

Then Samuel said to Jesse, "Are all your sons here?"
And he said, "There remains yet the youngest, but behold,
he is keeping the sheep." And Samuel said to Jesse, "Send
and get him, for we will not sit down till he comes here."
1 Samuel 16:11

My friend Charlie, an engineer, was always amazed at the uses of technology. One day he excitedly asked, "Stephen, can you believe that water can cut through steel and stone?" He handed me a little star carved from steel, and a delicate flower carved from stone. Each had been formed by plain water that was highly pressurized. Just ordinary water in skilled hands had done amazing things.

God does extraordinary things in his kingdom through ordinary people who are surrendered to Him. Every kind of person - shepherds, doctors, fisherman, tax collectors, business people, farmers – including you, can be used by God for His glory!

Lord God, I have no power on my own. Fill me with Your Holy Spirit today and use me for the sake of Your kingdom. Thank You that Your power works in and through me to bring You glory.

TUESDAY

"The time is fulfilled, and the kingdom of God is at hand; repent and believe in the gospel."

Mark 1:15

When Michele and I were dating, sometimes when it was late, her dad would say to me, "Stephen, you need to go home." Now, he said one thing, but he really meant two things. Because in order for me to go home, first, I had to leave his house – and that's probably what he was really after.

When the Bible talks about saving faith, it's really talking about two things. First, we have to repent, or turn, from our sinful life. Salvation without repentance is impossible. When you turn from sin, and then call on the name of Jesus, He will save you. So, have you first repented of your sin and then believed the gospel of Jesus Christ? That's how to be saved.

Lord Jesus, I believe that You died on the cross for my sin and that You rose from the grave. I don't want to continue to live in sin. By Your grace, save me, and I will follow You.

WEDNESDAY

*But you will receive power when the Holy Spirit
has come upon you, and you will be my witnesses
in Jerusalem and in all Judea and Samaria,
and to the end of the earth.*

Acts 1:8

I have the worst sense of direction in the whole world. My wife will tell you that when I go somewhere, I always go the worst possible route. But if you ask me how to get somewhere I've already been, I can tell you how to get there. I may not do it as well as Google Maps, but I can get you there.

A saved person can tell somebody else how to be saved. You may take a while to explain it to them, and they may need to ask you some questions. Your thoughts may be a little jumbled. You don't have to be an expert in the Bible to tell someone how to be saved. You just need to be a faithful witness.

Lord Jesus, I want to be Your witness. Thank You that the power to share the gospel doesn't come from me, but from Your Holy Spirit. Help me to be Your faithful witness wherever I go.

Thursday

Behold, he is coming with the clouds, and every eye will see him, even those who pierced him, and all tribes of the earth will wail on account of him. Even so. Amen.

Revelation 1:7

When I was in second grade, our teacher was very pregnant. She took two breaks every day, and each time she left the classroom, pandemonium erupted. The kids went crazy. A lookout was stationed at the door, and when he heard her in the hallway, he'd whisper loudly, "She's coming!" Then every kid in the room rushed to be on their best behavior.

The Bible says Jesus is coming. Are you ready? If you're not saved, today is the day for you to be saved; when Jesus gets here, it will be too late! If you are saved, are you living for Jesus? If not, now is the time to return to Him and live for His glory. Be ready; Jesus is coming soon!

Lord Jesus, help me to anticipate Your return every day. Where I'm not ready, help me to get ready. Help me to live a holy life while I wait for You and use me to help others get ready.

Friday

And they devoted themselves to the apostles' teaching and the fellowship, to the breaking of bread and the prayers.

Acts 2:42

In Edinburgh, Scotland, stands a statue to a little dog named Bobby. Bobby belonged to a policeman named John Gray. Bobby always accompanied his master on his daily rounds, until John Gray died in 1858. Even then, Bobby wouldn't leave John's side. Every night for fourteen years, Bobby devotedly slept by John's grave. The little dog was a picture of complete devotion.

Many people who call themselves Christians are not devoted to God. They're only interested in God. Devotion signifies a strong attachment, a commitment to something that you will not walk away from. How would you describe your devotion to Jesus? God is devoted to us, and Jesus is worthy of our highest devotion.

Lord God, You deserve my highest devotion – more than anyone or anything else in my life. Help me to purposely devote myself to Your Word, to prayer, and to obedience to You each day.

231

SATURDAY

With all humility and gentleness, with patience,
bearing with one another in love.
Ephesians 4:2

O ne time somebody said to me, "You know, it's easy for me to love people." And I just looked at him and said, "Have you met people?!" People can be hard to love; church people can be hard to love! But when we love Jesus, and are devoted to Him, He will help us to be devoted to each other in Christ's body.

The Bible shows that love isn't simply an emotion or a feeling; love involves action. Loving one another means to be compassionate and kind with one another. It means to forgive one another and to share with one another. Loving people – even hard to love people – invites God's blessing in our lives.

Lord Jesus, You have commanded me to love not just some peo-
ple, but all people. When I am offended and frustrated, give me
Your power to be patient and kind. Help me love like You love.

SUNDAY

*And day by day, attending the temple together
and breaking bread in their homes, they received
their food with glad and generous hearts.*

Acts 2:46

As a young preacher, I preached once a month in a nursing home. I had some doubts about whether God was really using me there because this one gentleman kept nodding off during my sermon! After the service was over, I went over to meet him. He said, "Preacher, I'm ninety-two years old. I can't hear a word you say." That's not what I wanted to hear! But then he said, "I come here every week because I want everybody to know whose side I'm on." I said, "Amen."

God blesses people who are devoted to worship, both in private and with the body of Christ. Corporate worship with the church blesses God's heart, and it encourages us. Don't miss opportunities to worship with your church.

———

*Lord Jesus, Thank You for adding me to Your church so that I
can live in community with other believers. As I am able, help
me to be with Your people to encourage them and be encouraged.*

MONDAY

The Spirit himself bears witness with
our spirit that we are children of God.
Romans 8:16

Once I arrived early to a meeting. As I was seated at the table, chairs started to fill up as people continued entering the room. Looking at the other people coming in, I felt like I didn't belong. These were people I admired. I felt they should be at the table, not me. When I stood and offered my seat, a good friend pulled me back down and said, "Stephen, you belong at this table."

You may feel that you don't belong at God's table. None of us deserve to be there because of our sin. Through faith in Jesus Christ and His blood shed on the cross, we become God's children. If you're a saved child of God, you belong at His table.

Father, You have given me a place of belonging with You and Your people. Help me to gladly welcome every person who belongs at Your table and to help them feel loved and accepted.

TUESDAY

*I know, O LORD, that the way of man is not in himself,
that it is not in man who walks to direct his steps.*
Jeremiah 10:23

Our little Yorkshire terrier, Joey, weighed less than five pounds. So when we would walk Joey, his tiny legs required thousands of steps just to keep up. Joey got distracted by other dogs, smells, and sounds. That's why we used a leash with Joey. It made us able to correct him and keep him on the path he needed to be on.

In a similar way, it is the Lord who orders our steps. While we may make our plans, God determines how our plans will work out! Don't strain against the directing hand of God on your life. Trust Him; his way for you is always best.

---

*Lord, I ask for Your wisdom to help me to plan well for the days
and years of my life. But give me grace to hold my plans loosely
and to follow the steps that You sovereignly ordain for me.*

WEDNESDAY

Pray without ceasing.
1 Thessalonians 5:17

Imagine you're traveling with a friend from Florida to California. Being confined in the car with your friend over several days would surely result in a lot of conversation. Now, what if you make the entire road trip in silence? You keep your thoughts to yourself and sit quietly. That would suggest one of two things – you either don't really know your friend very well, or you don't like him at all.

A healthy relationship with Jesus should have us talking to Him throughout the day. If we're not talking with Jesus regularly, we either don't know Him very well, or we don't really love Him. So remember today to be in constant communication with Jesus. When you do that, you will also love Jesus more.

Lord Jesus, help me to live in an atmosphere of prayer, where talking to You is as natural as breathing. Thank You that communicating with You isn't confined to just my quiet time.

THURSDAY

*Likewise the Spirit helps us in our weakness.
For we do not know what to pray for as we ought,
but the Spirit himself intercedes for us with
groanings too deep for words.*

Romans 8:26

When I was on a mission trip in El Salvador, we went to a fast-food restaurant for dinner. I recognized the pictures on the menu, but I didn't understand any of the words. So when it was my turn to order, I was nervous because I didn't know enough Spanish to ask for a hamburger. But my friend, who speaks great Spanish, stepped up and ordered for me. He was able to use just the right words to order my food.

That's how the Holy Spirit intercedes for us in prayer. He asks the Father for exactly what we need according to God's will. We often don't know the right words to pray, but the Holy Spirit, our helper, always does.

Father, Thank You that Your Holy Spirit speaks to You on my behalf. I'm glad that I can't mess up my prayers, because the Holy Spirit straightens them out and prays for me, just the right way.

FRIDAY

For you yourselves are fully aware that the day
of the Lord will come like a thief in the night.
1 Thessalonians 5:2

When I was a little boy in second grade, thieves broke into our home. Then, when Michele and I had been married for about eight or nine years, some thieves broke into our home. And you know what? Neither time did the thief call ahead of time to tell us that he was coming.

The Bible says that when Jesus Christ returns, His coming will be like a thief in the night. He will come suddenly and on a day we don't expect. But it shouldn't catch you by surprise. Jesus has told us that He will return. He has given us time to be prepared. So be watchful and ready, because Jesus could come today.

Lord Jesus, I know that Your coming will be sudden. I don't want to be unready when You appear. Help me to prepare my heart every day to see You and to live every day expecting You.

SATURDAY

*So then let us not sleep, as others do,
but let us keep awake and be sober.*
1 Thessalonians 5:6

The city of Norfolk, Virginia, entered into a multi-million-dollar contract with a security company to guard over three plots of property. The security was lax; the guards on duty were often found watching television. Many times they were found sleeping on the job. So the city cancelled the contract based on this: a guard ought to guard!

God calls us to be watchful because Jesus is coming! It's not time for us to be asleep. It's not time for us to be distracted. It's not time for us to stop loving our neighbors. As we wait for Christ's return, let's be awake and about His kingdom business, always being ready for Jesus.

God, help me to be spiritually alert, watching and waiting every day for the return of Jesus Christ. Help me to not grow weary, but to be faithfully serving You when You arrive.

Sunday

*Abide in me, and I in you. As the branch cannot
bear fruit by itself, unless it abides in the vine,
neither can you, unless you abide in me.*

John 15:4

Years ago Michele and I had a friend we loved having over. But we knew that when she came over, she would stay and stay. You could yawn and say, "It's really getting late," but she'd just answer, "It sure is," and stay where she was. We finally learned to relax and enjoy the visit until she was ready to go.

When you spend time with Jesus, He's not going to lean up on His seat and look at His watch. He won't tell you about the other things He needs to get to. He won't say, "Hey, time for you to leave!" He loves time with you, and you need to be with Him. Abide in Jesus, and He promises to abide in You.

---

*Lord Jesus, there is no life apart from You, and I can't be fruitful
unless I abide in You. Help me to stay close to You every day so
You can produce Your good fruit in me.*

MONDAY

I am the vine; you are the branches. Whoever abides in me and I in him, he it is that bears much fruit, for apart from me you can do nothing.
John 15:5

Have you ever had a guest who can't stay? You know – the person who tells you as soon as he walks in, "Hey it's good to see you, but I really can't stay." I'm thinking, "Why did you come if you're too busy to stay? Maybe you should have just stayed home."

Sometimes we're like that with Jesus. Jesus wants you to be like the guest who won't leave! The one who says, "I want to be here with you because I love you. I want to keep talking with you and listening to you." Don't be too busy to spend time with Jesus. Abide with Him through His Word and prayer. The fruitful Christian is the abiding Christian.

Lord Jesus, I confess that sometimes I brush You off to do other things. Grow my desire to be with You and to hear Your voice. Help me to learn more each day what it means to abide in You.

Tuesday

*Every branch in me that does not bear fruit he
takes away, and every branch that does bear fruit he
prunes, that it may bear more fruit.*
John 15:2

A vinedresser's responsibility is the health of the grape-
vine. Sometimes it's necessary to pinch off the end
of a branch that seems to be growing well. If a branch is
diseased, or growing in a wrong direction, the vinedresser will pinch back a portion of the branch to help it be
healthy and productive. It slows things down for a while,
but it's best for the branch.

God is always working, even when life seems to be at
a standstill. As we abide in Jesus, sometimes God "pinch-
es us back" to make us spiritually healthy and productive.
The vinedresser knows what he's doing. Everything He
does is to help the vine be fruitful. So keep abiding; God
will make you fruitful.

---

*God, You know best what's required for my life to produce good
fruit. Though it's painful, I surrender today to whatever You
have to pinch back in my life to make me fruitful for You.*

WEDNESDAY

Whoever keeps his commandments abides in God, and God in him. And by this we know that he abides in us, by the Spirit whom he has given us.

1 John 3:24

I'm really fair-skinned, so I wear sunscreen when I plan to be outside. But if I'm outside for a while unexpectedly, I'll get sunburned. When that happens, I don't have to tell anybody that I've been in the sun. They can tell.

How can you tell if you're abiding in Jesus? You'll keep His commandments! Apart from abiding in Jesus Christ, you can do nothing that's really important to God. But when you abide in Him He will enable you to do all kinds of things beyond what you can imagine. He'll produce fruit in your life you can't produce on your own. When you abide in Jesus, and He abides in you, you can tell, and so can others.

_____

Lord Jesus, obeying Your commandments is the evidence that I'm abiding in You. Help me to obey Your commandments so that Your fruit will grow in me.

Thursday

And I will ask the Father, and he will give you another Helper, to be with you forever.
John 14:16

Bible translators had difficulty finding a word in a tribal language for *helper.* But they saw that when groups of tribal men headed into the bush carrying large loads, there was always one man who carried nothing. They thought he must be the boss. But they were told, "Oh no; when someone falls down under the load, he helps them get back up again." They called him a word that meant *the one who falls down beside us.* It was exactly the word the translators needed.

God's Holy Spirit is our helper. He picks us up when we stumble under the weight of our burdens. He gives strength so we can keep going. God never leaves us without a helper.

Father, help me to walk in the power of the Holy Spirit today so that I can faithfully love and serve You. I'm so thankful that You've given me a Helper to be able to follow and obey You.

FRIDAY

Peace I leave with you; my peace I give to you.
Not as the world gives do I give to you. Let not your
hearts be troubled, neither let them be afraid.
John 14:27

My mom prays for me. Once I told her, "Mom, I've got some things that are causing me a lot of stress. Pray for God to remove those things from my life." Her answer surprised me. She said, "No, Son, I won't pray for that. I will ask God to give you His peace in the midst of the stress." It's not what I asked for, but my mom did pray what was very best for me.

Sometimes God does remove our stresses, but most often He wants us to learn to trust Him in difficult situations. As we learn to trust Jesus, we experience His peace that transcends our circumstances. "Let not your heart be troubled" is only possible when you trust God.

Lord, I've never experienced real peace apart from You. When my heart is troubled, help me to turn my eyes upon Jesus and experience Your peace, even if my circumstances do not change.

Saturday

*Abide in me, and I in you. As the branch cannot
bear fruit by itself, unless it abides in the vine,
neither can you, unless you abide in me.*
John 15:4

My grandfather lived out in the country, where he grew muscadines, which are like grapes. One day I went out to pick some muscadines to eat, and I heard lots of loud creaking and groaning. I realized the vine was making the noise. I asked, "What are you doing?" And the vine said, "I'm trying hard to produce fruit and push a muscadine out on this branch."

That silly story makes a good point: a branch isn't responsible for bearing the fruit; that's the vine's job. The vine produces fruit on the branches that are connected to it. Are you abiding in Jesus today? He always produces fruit when we stay connected to Him.

---

*Lord Jesus, You produce fruit in me; my only responsibility is
to obey You. Give me grace today to obey You so that my life is
not fruitless, but abundantly fruitful.*

SUNDAY

And they were singing a new song before the throne and before the four living creatures and before the elders. No one could learn that song except the 144,000 who had been redeemed from the earth.

Revelation 14:3

There are some musical artists I really like, and I love to sing their songs in the car, or when I'm working outside. In fact, I have many of those songs memorized. It's almost like they're my songs, but they're not. Each of those songs belongs to someone else.

Every person redeemed by Jesus Christ has a distinct song to sing! We're all saved the same way, by the grace of God and the blood of His Son Jesus Christ, but each story of God's grace in our lives is unique. We can give our songs back to God in praise, and we can tell them to other people for their encouragement. Tell *your* grace story to someone today. God will use it for His glory!

Lord Jesus, Your salvation gives me a song about the gospel and about my testimony of Your grace to me. Help me to share my song of Your grace with someone who needs to hear it today.

MONDAY

Speak to all the congregation of the people of
Israel and say to them, You shall be holy,
for I the LORD your God am holy.
Leviticus 19:2

A page of a child's magazine had four simple drawings.
Three were of oranges, and one was of an apple. The
question at the bottom was, "Which one is different?" Well,
even the smallest child can pick out the one that's different.

Followers of Jesus are not called to be isolated from
the world, but to be separate from the world. That's what it
means for us to be holy; we're to be different! We shouldn't
look, sound, or act like lost people. Instead, we should look
like Jesus. Would your family, friends, and neighbors pick
you out as the one who's different because of Jesus Christ?
Let's strive to be holy because the Lord our God is holy.

Lord God, You are holy; there is no one like You. Because You
are my Father, I should look like You. Help me to bear the im-
age of Your Son Jesus Christ by living a holy life.

TUESDAY

I write these things to you who believe in the name of the Son of God, that you may know that you have eternal life.

1 John 5:13

That great preacher, C. H. Spurgeon, is quoted as saying that he was so sure of his salvation that he could grab onto a cornstalk and swing out over the fires of Hell into the face of the devil, and sing, "Blessed assurance! Jesus is mine." That's confidence!

If you've turned from your sin and are trusting in Jesus Christ alone for your salvation, you don't have to hope that you're saved; you can *know* that you're saved. Jesus Christ did everything that needs to be done for you to be saved when He died on the cross for your sins and rose from the grave. If you know you've been saved, you've been saved forever.

Lord Jesus, I want to stand upon Your promise that because I believe in Your name, I can know for certain that I have eternal life. Thank You for the assurance of my salvation.

WEDNESDAY

*You shall tell your son on that day, "It is because of
what the LORD did for me when I came out of Egypt."*
Exodus 13:8

Michael Reagan, son of President Ronald Reagan, described what he said was the greatest gift a child can
receive. He said, "When my father closed his eyes in death,
that's when I realized the gift that my dad gave to me. Back
in 1988, he had told me about his love of God and his love
of Christ as His Savior." He said, "I didn't know what it all
meant then, but I do now. I can't think of a better gift for a
father to give a son."

Don't leave your family guessing about where you're
going to spend eternity. Make sure *you* know that you're
saved, then make sure your family knows. There's no greater gift you can give them.

---

*Lord Jesus, I want my testimony to bless my family. Help me to
create a legacy of faith and to share my faith in Jesus with them.
Lord Jesus, save my children and grandchildren.*

THURSDAY

For to set the mind on the flesh is death, but to set the mind on the Spirit is life and peace.

Romans 8:6

Our son Joshua was about eight years old when Michele and I gave in and got him a pair of gerbils. He named them Oreo and Snickerdoodle. I soon saw my parents' wisdom in refusing to get me gerbils when I was a kid. Even in the middle of the night tthe gerbils kept the wheel in their cage spinning – clickety, clickety, clickety. Oreo and Snickerdoodle never stopped. They were on the go, seemingly frantic all the time.

God has much more for you than constant, frantic activity with no real purpose. God wants to give you real peace. Fill your mind with God's Word, and trust Him. When you do, God promises to give you, not just quiet, but perfect peace.

Father, You promise peace when I set my mind on You. Help me to be intentional about quietly setting my mind on You so I can experience the peace that You have for me.

Friday

*This is the message we have heard from him
and proclaim to you, that God is light,
and in him is no darkness at all.*

1 John 1:5

A young man and his mom were talking about his day, when he suddenly asked, "Mom, what's the world going to be like when I'm an adult? There's so much darkness and confusion, I can't even imagine what it's going to be like in twenty years."

That young man was right: the world is dark. But wherever Jesus is there will be light, because Jesus is the light of the world. Light has only one message for darkness: Get out! So no matter what the future holds, if Jesus is there – and He will always be with His people - He will bring light to the darkness. That's really good news!

Lord Jesus, help me not to fear the future. I don't know what awaits me, but You do, and You are already there. Thank You that because You are light, darkness can never overwhelm me.

SATURDAY

The heavens declare the glory of God,
and the sky above proclaims his handiwork.
Psalm 19:1

Watch reality TV and you'll see people pursuing their life-goals. Some of them are mining for gold, or cooking with things most of us would never eat, or trying to find the perfect house, even the perfect spouse. Reality television shows us a very edited clip of real life. And the cast of players rarely finds lasting satisfaction.

God is the author of reality. Christians need a Bible-based way of understanding, interpreting, and living in the world. Anything in our lives that doesn't correspond to what God says in His Word is not only deficient, but wrong. Let's strive to have a God-centered worldview in every area of our lives. Then we can live confidently and with wisdom in the real world.

God, I want to have a God-centered, biblical view of the world
and everything in it. Help me to think like You think about
everything, so that I can live with wisdom in these trying days.

SUNDAY

More to be desired are they than gold,
even much fine gold; sweeter also than honey
and drippings of the honeycomb.
Psalm 19:10

A book collector paid $47,000 for one leaf from a five-hundred-year-old Guttenberg Bible, renowned as the first book ever printed. The collector valued his purchase greatly and treated his one leaf of the antiquated Bible with great respect. He couldn't read it, however, because the text is printed in Latin. It was still God's Word, but it didn't change anything about him.

What value do you place on your Bible? God doesn't intend for your Bible to only be on display. He intends for your thoughts, actions, and who you are to be shaped by its truth. The great value of your Bible isn't in what you believe *about* it, but in how it changes your life.

God, your Word is powerful to change my life.
Help me to treasure Your Word, to know it, and obey it
so that I can walk in Your way and be pleasing to You.

MONDAY

Let the words of my mouth and the meditation
of my heart be acceptable in your sight,
O LORD, my rock and my redeemer.
Psalm 19:14

As a child, I could memorize things easily. Now that I'm older, memorizing anything is a challenge! So when I read my Bible, I'll pick one verse to memorize, and I'll work on it for that day. I may not remember it tomorrow, but even if I only remember it for today, it helps me today.

Not even age is an excuse to avoid memorizing God's Word! If you can memorize a verse for even one hour, it does you good for that hour. And as you do your best to meditate on and remember Scripture, it will help you move forward in living to please God in every part of your life.

———————————

Father, I know that my speech reflects the condition of my heart. So help me to meditate upon Your Word so that my heart, the words of my mouth, and every part of my life are transformed.

Tuesday

*The precepts of the LORD are right,
rejoicing the heart; the commandment of
the LORD is pure, enlightening the eyes.*

Psalm 19:8

I heard about a guy whose resume included all of this: husband; dad; military strategist; agriculturist; survivalist; outdoorsman; friend; fearless leader; politician; inspirational speaker; poet; musician; administrator; and diplomat. This impressive man was David, the king of Israel. If you asked David, "How do you divide up what you believe about God and how you live your life in all these different areas?" he'd have said, "I don't! What I believe about God transforms every area of my life – even when I mess up badly."

Don't try to govern each different area of your life by a separate set of rules. God gives us one life that is best lived when His truth shapes and transforms every part of it.

———————————

Father, help me to filter every issue in my life and in this world through Your Word. Your Word is always right; it is always pure. It will never change. Your Word is the authority in my life.

WEDNESDAY

For the Son of Man came to seek and to save the lost.
Luke 19:10

A little girl wandered away from home and became lost. Her parents and grandparents, neighbors, and even the police searched through the woods near her home for hours, looking for their precious little girl. They searched through the night, and just as the sun was rising, they saw her, sitting on a stump, crying and cold. When her dad swooped her up in his arms, she cried, "Oh Daddy, I found you!"

You may feel that when you got saved, you found Jesus. The Bible says that nobody seeks after God. So God sent His Son Jesus to find lost people and save them. Are you still lost? Jesus is seeking you today. That's how important you are to God.

Lord Jesus, Thank You that when I would not look for You, You sought me and saved me. Thank You that You're still seeking and saving lost people. Please save my lost friends and family!

Thursday

*And when Jesus came to the place, he looked up
and said to him, "Zacchaeus, hurry and come down,
for I must stay at your house today."*
Luke 19:5

I was telling the story of Zacchaeus to a group of second graders one day, and I asked, "How did Jesus know Zacchaeus's name?" A little boy sitting on the front row answered, "Because He's Jesus! Jesus knows everybody's name." That was the best thing anybody said during my Bible lesson that day.

Jesus knows your name. Not only that, but He knows absolutely everything about you. Jesus knows your failures, your guilt, and your secrets. He knows your hurts and how you've hurt others. Even so, He still loves you with all the love of His heart. Jesus wants to save you. Will you invite Him into your life today?

---

*Lord Jesus, Thank You for loving me and calling my name.
Lord Jesus, I welcome You into the home of my heart. Please
forgive my sin and save me, Jesus. I want to follow You.*

Friday

And Zacchaeus stood and said to the Lord, "Behold, Lord, the half of my goods I give to the poor. And if I have defrauded anyone of anything, I restore it fourfold."
Luke 19:8

I keep a close eye on the gas gauge in my car. If it's pointing toward Empty, I know that I need to fill up soon, or I won't be going anywhere. In fact, I like to always keep the needle pointed toward Full.

The way you treat your money and possessions, how generous you are, and how honest you are, are good indicators of whether Jesus Christ has really done a work in your heart. Jesus said that Zacchaeus' open-handedness was evidence that salvation had truly come to Zacchaeus. Is the needle of generosity and honesty pointed toward F or E in your life? It's a gauge you shouldn't ignore.

Lord, help me not to hoard money and possessions for my pleasure but to use them generously as a tool to build Your kingdom. Help me to hold wealth loosely and to be honest with money.

SATURDAY

And Zacchaeus stood and said to the Lord, "Behold, Lord, the half of my goods I give to the poor. And if I have defrauded anyone of anything, I restore it fourfold."
Luke 19:8

The Old Testament law said that if you had stolen anything, you were required to give back what you had taken, plus one fifth. If you had stolen a dollar, you were required to give back a dollar and twenty cents. But when the cheating tax collector Zacchaeus met Jesus, he said, "If I've taken a dollar from somebody, I'll give them back four dollars." Now that's a changed life.

You are important to Jesus. He never leaves us like He finds us! When Jesus saves you, He changes how you treat people. He changes your attitudes, your priorities, and your desires. Have you been saved? Only if you've been changed.

Lord, search my heart and show me if I lack integrity in any part of my life. Where there is sin, I want to make it right. Help my life to reflect the character of Jesus Christ.

Sunday

And when he comes home, he calls together his friends
and his neighbors, saying to them, "Rejoice with me,
for I have found my sheep that was lost."
Luke 15:6

A distraught daughter couldn't find her mother's wedding ring in the hospital room where she had died. The hospital CEO promised he would do all he could to find the ring. They searched the room carefully, but the ring remained lost. Unwilling to give up, the CEO went to the hospital laundry. He plunged his hand into a basket of wet, dirty sheets. Amazingly, he found the ring.

Lost isn't an ugly word; *lost* is a beautiful word. When God says that you're lost, He doesn't mean that you're worthless, but that you're precious and worth finding. God gave His Son Jesus Christ to die on the cross to pay for your sins with His own blood. That's how valuable you are to God.

Lord Jesus, that You would pay for my sins with Your
blood shows me how valuable my soul is to You.
Thank You for finding me, for rescuing me with
your own blood, and for rejoicing over me.

MONDAY

And he was seeking to see who Jesus was,
but on account of the crowd he could not,
because he was small in stature.

Luke 19:3

Zacchaeus was a wee little man. You may know the song. But Zacchaeus wasn't just wee in stature. He was wee in character. He was wee in likeability. Zacchaeus was wee in many ways. He probably never entertained the hope that God would love him. Zacchaeus was lost.

But Jesus said that He came to seek and to save that which was lost. That was Jesus' mission statement. Jesus spoke those very words to a man who spent most of his life thinking he wasn't important. He didn't matter. Nobody cared. No one liked him. When Jesus found Zacchaeus and changed his life, it proved that everyone – including you – is important to God.

———————

Lord Jesus, I praise You that my life matters to You so much
that You died on the cross to pay the price for my sin. Thank
You for saving me and for giving my life meaning.

Tuesday

Saying, "Father, if you are willing, remove this cup from me. Nevertheless, not my will, but yours, be done."
Luke 22:42

When I was a teenager, I always loved it when my dad would take my car out for a drive. He noticed things I didn't. One time he said, "Son, your car pulls to the right. I have to fight the steering wheel when I drive it. You need to have your wheels aligned."

Maybe you need an alignment today – not a *wheel* alignment, but a *will* alignment. Don't pull against God's will for your life. Jesus won the victory over sin and death for you and me through complete surrender. Surrender is always the path to victory for the believer. To win, we must surrender to God's will, just like Jesus.

_____

God, thank You for the complete surrender of Jesus to Your plan to save me. Give me grace to humbly surrender to Your perfect will for me, knowing it is always best, even when it's hard.

WEDNESDAY

*So Jesus said to Peter, "Put your sword
into its sheath; shall I not drink the cup
that the Father has given me?"*
John 18:11

One day I answered the phone and heard my friend Tim's voice. With great sadness he said that his oldest nephew had been killed in an accident. Tim, who is a pastor, was so burdened. He said, "I've always preached about trust in the Lord. But this is so hard." He was devastated, but knew that God was somehow working, even in this time of desolation for his family.

Every believer must follow Jesus to Gethsemane. Great distress in our lives tills the soil of total surrender to God, who is always good. In great sorrow, Jesus entrusted Himself to God, and so can we. Our deepest sorrows lead us to trust completely in God, and there we find Him to be good.

---

*Lord Jesus, You do not call me to anything You've
not first endured Yourself. You know firsthand
about sorrow. Help me to entrust every hard thing
to You, knowing that You fully understand.*

THURSDAY

If we confess our sins, he is faithful and just to forgive us our sins and to cleanse us from all unrighteousness.
1 John 1:9

I heard of a young man who went into a store and asked to change a dollar bill into four quarters. Then he went to another store and asked to change that for ten dimes. Then he went to another store and got twenty nickels. Then he went to the next store and got a hundred pennies. Somebody asked, "Why are you doing this?" He replied, "One of these times, somebody's going to make a mistake, and it's not going to be me."

We all sin and make mistakes. As followers of Jesus, God is always faithful to forgive your sin. God is gracious, and loves you when you confess your sin to Him.

_____

God, Thank You for Your mercy and forgiveness when I confess my sin to You. Your blood is powerful to cleanse me today, just as on the day that You saved me. I'm grateful for Your blood!

FRIDAY

Turn in the account of your management,
for you can no longer be manager.

Luke 16:2

My friend Wiley, a communications company execu-
tive, told me that sometimes an employee would cost
the company thousands of dollars through an honest mistake, but keep their job. Others were fired for stealing quarters from public telephones. Why get fired over twenty-five
cents? They showed they couldn't be trusted.

Jesus wants to entrust us with great blessings. But He
requires us to be trustworthy with what He's already given
us. You must be faithful in small things before Jesus entrusts
you with greater things.

Father, help me to not stiff-arm people who are different from
me, but in whom you are working to build Your kingdom. I
want a heart of humility.

SATURDAY

I have fought the good fight, I have
finished the race, I have kept the faith.
2 Timothy 4:7

A s kids, my friends and I loved watching professional wrestling on Saturdays. We always debated the same question: Was it real? Were those wrestlers really fighting each other, or was it all just a show?

It's childish to watch an imaginary fight, thinking it's real; but it's dangerous to be in a real fight, thinking it's imaginary! Christians wrestle everyday against the sinful forces of the world, temptations of our flesh, and attacks from our spiritual enemy, the devil.

Through Jesus, you can fight the good fight. He will empower you today to face evil and win as you trust in Him.

Lord Jesus, make me aware of the spiritual battle
around me. Empower me by Your Holy Spirit to stand
against Satan's attempts to make me ineffective for You.
Help me to finish my race well.

Sunday

Brothers, do not be children in your thinking.
Be infants in evil, but in your thinking be mature.
1 Corinthians 14:20

It is so important to be mature in our thinking. The spiritually immature person is often tossed about by emotion, and that can be miserable. As we navigate the political and societal storms around us,, we must be guided by God's truth, and not our feelings.

Are you looking to God through His Word and prayer, or being emotionally tossed about by today's news? Becoming a mature follower of Jesus Christ will build a firm foundation of joy that is greater than both your feelings and your circumstances. Our feelings can be up and down and all over the place. God is always faithful and trustworthy. We can trust God.

Father, I want to mature in my faith in You. Help me to do the work of studying, learning, and obeying Your Word so that I can practice the things that will grow my faith in Jesus Christ.

Monday

Not that I am speaking of being in need, for I have learned in whatever situation I am to be content.
Philippians 4:11

It's a pretty big claim for someone to say, "I'm content, no matter what." You might say, "Well Paul never lived through a global pandemic. He didn't have to deal with soaring inflation. Paul never faced cancer." But you know what? Paul experienced long seasons of social distancing, financial hardship, and even illness.

Paul learned real contentment by living every day in the power of Jesus Christ. He learned to trust the faithful love of God, in every situation – the good and the bad - so that he could say, "I'm good, I'm content," no matter what the day brought.

What's happening in your life today? No matter your circumstances, in Jesus Christ you can experience true contentment.

———————

Father, I have peace with You in Jesus Christ. You'll never leave me, and eternal life can't be taken from me. I need nothing more than to be content. Help me to choose contentment today.

TUESDAY

*And he said to his disciples, "Therefore I tell you,
do not be anxious about your life, what you will eat,
nor about your body, what you will put on."*
Luke 12:22

I confess that I tend to worry. Sometimes I try to justify my worry as a weakness. I think, "well, this is just how I'm wired." But God's Word says that worry isn't just weakness. Worry is sin because Jesus has commanded me not to worry.

I'm so glad Jesus paid the price for my worry when He died on the cross. And now, His resurrection from the grave empowers me to overcome worry in my life. When you walk by faith, Jesus will give you the power to conquer worry. He always gives grace and power to help us obey what He commands and to keep moving forward.

---

*Lord Jesus, I confess my worry to You right now. Lord, give me
Your grace to turn from worry, and to count every concern as an
opportunity to see You work and provide.*

WEDNESDAY

Look at the birds of the air: they neither sow nor reap nor gather into barns, and yet your heavenly Father feeds them. Are you not of more value than they?
Matthew 6:26

Someone has calculated that there are between two hundred and four hundred *billion* wild birds living on earth right now. They have to eat every day. God feeds every one of them, not just for one day, or for a week. He feeds them three hundred sixty-five days a year, year after year after year.

In these difficult days we're living in, remember that you are more valuable to God than the birds! In other words, if God takes care of the birds, He'll take care of you. He'll meet every need you have, every day of your life. God loves you, and you can trust Him to care for you.

Heavenly Father, make the birds a reminder to me that I can trust You to meet all of my needs. You have provided for me until this very day, and You will never stop taking good care of me.

THURSDAY

And he said to them, "Come away by yourselves to a desolate place and rest a while." For many were coming and going, and they had no leisure even to eat.

Mark 6:31

In our busy culture, we're occasionally made to feel guilty for taking time away from our work. Vacation time goes unclaimed. Work hours pile up. It seems we can never get caught up. One thing we can't afford to let slide is real rest. Jesus gives us permission to occasionally step away from our work for a few days for some rest and relaxation.

Sometimes we need to rest for health reasons. Rest also helps us keep up our guard against our weaknesses. We occasionally need down-time to reconnect with our families and build relationships. We also need restful times to reflect on God's work in our lives. Don't ignore your need for rest. It might be just what the Great Physician orders!

Thank You, Lord Jesus, for Your provision of rest when I'm weary. Help me to not ignore my need to stop and rest. I will trust You to meet my needs when I take time to rest.

Friday

*For what does it profit a man to gain
the whole world and forfeit his soul?*
Mark 8:36

What is your most valuable possession? Your bank account? A piece of jewelry or art? Maybe it's your house or your car. Everyone owns something infinitely more valuable than any of those things. Nothing is more valuable than your soul. If you lose your soul, you've lost everything.

Your soul is so valuable that Jesus willingly paid the only price acceptable to God to redeem you. He gave His own life for yours. Jesus took every painful step to Calvary, where Roman soldiers nailed Him to a cross. He suffered and bled for six torturous hours to pay the high price for our sins so we could have eternal life.

The cost to redeem us was tremendous. We could never pay it, but Jesus already has. That's all the proof you need to know that God loves you.

———————

Father, without Jesus, my soul would be eternally lost. I praise You for valuing me so highly that You paid the highest price to redeem me. Thank You for loving me so much.

Saturday

For we do not have a high priest who is unable to sympathize with our weaknesses, but one who in every respect has been tempted as we are, yet without sin.
Hebrews 4:15

When you suffer, who do you want in the room with you? Most likely someone who's been through the same thing and knows exactly what you're going through.

That's the kind of comforter Jesus is when we suffer. He became like us in *every* way. He endured everything we endure. Jesus experienced rejection, pain, loss, and separation. He experienced those things, and never sinned. Jesus knows exactly how to comfort us in our deepest pain.

Whatever you're going through right now, Jesus has already been there. He knows your pain. He knows exactly how to help you through it.

———————

Lord Jesus, because You suffered, You completely understand my pain. Help me to hear Your voice of comfort in my sorrows. Then show me who I can share Your comfort with.

SUNDAY

No temptation has overtaken you that is not common to man. God is faithful, and he will not let you be tempted beyond your ability, but with the temptation he will also provide the way of escape, that you may be able to endure it.

1 Corinthians 10:13

Sometimes I see photos of people flirting with dangerous ledges, seeing how close they can get to the edge without falling. Sadly, some lose their balance and fall to a tragic end. They didn't mean for disaster to happen, but it was one hundred percent avoidable if they had kept away from the edge.

It is always foolish to flirt with temptation to see just how close we can get to sin without giving in.

God has a word for you: Run! Get as far away from the temptation as you can and do it as fast as you can. Slipping over the edge and falling into sin can destroy your life. God always provides a way of escape when we're tempted. Ask God to help you find the way of escape, so you can avoid sin and the pain that always comes with it.

Father, fill me with Your Spirit so that I recognize temptation. Help me to search for the way of escape instead of trying to get as close to sin as I can without getting caught. I don't want to fall!

MONDAY

*Look carefully then how you walk, not as
unwise but as wise, making the best use of
the time, because the days are evil.*

Ephesians 5:15–16

Time and people are both precious. Sometimes we waste
time on insignificant stuff instead of investing in people for God's glory.

How might your schedule need tweaking to best use
the time God gives you for His kingdom? It may be as simple as turning off the TV, or putting your phone down. You
can then spend a few extra minutes in your Bible, or with
your family, or checking on someone at church.

Be careful and wise with both your time and your relationships. They are two of God's best gifts.

---

*God, Thank You for Your good gift of time. Help me to use
time wisely to grow my relationships with You and others. Help
me not to waste time on distractions that profit me nothing.*

TUESDAY

Be sober-minded; be watchful. Your adversary
the devil prowls around like a roaring lion,
seeking someone to devour.

1 Peter 5:8

Magicians can't really saw people in two. But what they are really good at is getting you to redirect your focus onto something else so they can create an illusion. They're not really magicians, but masters of misdirection.

The devil works really hard to make you redirect your attention away from Jesus Christ – not so he can play a harmless trick on you, but so he can destroy you. We are to be always focused and watchful with our eyes on Jesus. That's how to resist the devil's tricks of discouragement, temptation, and lies that can easily defeat us. Remember, Jesus in you is greater than the devil and his deception.

Father, keep me mindful of the enemy's evil intentions, but help
me to keep my eyes on Jesus. He defeated the enemy at the
cross, so the devil has no power over me when I abide in You.

WEDNESDAY

Therefore I tell you, whatever you ask in prayer,
believe that you have received it, and it will be yours.
Mark 11:24

A little boy wanted badly to fly like Superman. He prayed for God to help him. Then, in faith, he climbed onto a chair, and jumped from it as high as he could. His best effort at having faith couldn't keep him from thumping back onto the ground, disappointed.

God's promise to answer prayer isn't a blank check to give us whatever we can dream up. Our requests of God must be filtered through His expressed will, revealed in His Word. When you pray in faith *and* according to His will, God is willing to do what we can't even imagine! So don't be bashful about asking God for the impossible. He really can move mountains.

Father, You give me authority to pray big prayers! I trust You to
hear and to answer my prayers because nothing is impossible for
You. Help me to always pray surrendered to Your will.

THURSDAY

I will instruct you and teach you in the way you should go; I will counsel you with my eye upon you.
Psalm 32:8

A friend who spent his life as a teacher told me about a student who paid him a visit one afternoon. My friend was known as a tough instructor. Students complained about how hard his course was. But this student didn't come to ask for easier assignments. Instead, he said, "Don't stop pushing us. We know you see something great in us that we can't see yet."

Our God is the greatest teacher. He works constantly to instruct you. You may not always enjoy the assignments He gives you, but His eye is on you. God works in every circumstance to make His vision for your life a reality as you follow Jesus.

Father, I praise You for being my guide through life. You've promised to teach me through Your Word and through prayer so that I don't go the wrong way when I follow You. Thank You!

FRIDAY

*Do you not know that in a race all the
runners run, but only one receives the prize?
So run that you may obtain it.*
1 Corinthians 9:24

Recently, my family visited an athletic stadium in Athens, Greece, where runners competed during Paul's time. I learned something surprising. On ancient racetracks, runners ran in a straight line, to a post at the end of the course, then turned and ran back. The runners went back and forth until they finished their race.

That's a great picture of the Christian life. We cover the same spiritual ground over and over, facing the same daily challenges, seeking to trust God in the same simple areas. Daily faithfulness to Jesus is the way to win the race.

---

*Father, Thank You for opportunities to trust You again and again
and build my spiritual muscles. Help me to run my race faithfully
and to not be spiritually lazy. I want to finish my race well.*

SATURDAY

In the day of prosperity be joyful, and in the day of adversity consider: God has made the one as well as the other, so that man may not find out anything that will be after him.

Ecclesiastes 7:14

It's a simple but life-changing principle: Our God makes every day. He makes days when we get good news — like the birth of a new grandchild or the promotion your spouse had been hoping for. He makes the days when we get devastating news like a doctor's message that the test came back positive for cancer.

When you trust that God is in control of every day, whether good or bad, you can also be sure that His wisdom will guide you and His grace will sustain you through every day. No matter what your day holds, your God still holds the day!

_____

Lord God, You bless me with good things that I don't deserve. You are faithful when life is hard. You are good all the time. Help me to learn well the lessons of both prosperity and adversity.

Sunday

*So Noah went out, and his sons and his
wife and his sons' wives with him.*
Genesis 8:18

You know the story: Noah and his family were cooped up in the ark for more than a year, where they rode out the storm and then waited for the water to recede. The wait was tough, but it was absolutely the only way for them to trust God and experience His plan.

If you're tired of your present situation, and eager to take the next steps, but you find that the Lord wants you to wait, don't be discouraged. His plans for us require patience, faith, and obedience. It may seem contradictory, but moving forward with Jesus sometimes requires standing still.

———

Lord God, I know that learning patience requires waiting, sometimes for a really long time. Help me to learn to wait for You well, being faithful to You, and trusting Your faithfulness to me.

MONDAY

Let the wise hear and increase in learning,
and the one who understands obtain guidance.
Proverbs 1:5

A favorite uncle asked his little eight-year-old niece how her second-grade year in school had been. "Did you learn a lot?" he asked. "Yes," she confidently answered. "I know just about everything there is to know!"

Well, none of us knows everything. We need others to help us learn, to give us wise counsel, and to give us a loving warning when we're about to run off the rails. We *all* need godly counselors. They should be those who know God's Word and obey it themselves. Listen to them carefully, and allow God to speak to you through them. God will use them to help you find the right way.

Lord God, You say that even the wise and understanding have a lot to learn. Help me to not trust my own knowledge or wisdom, but to continually seek Yours. I will never reach the end of it!

Tuesday

Though you have not seen him, you love him. Though you do not now see him, you believe in him and rejoice with joy that is inexpressible and filled with glory.

1 Peter 1:8

An eighty-year-old golfer with failing eyesight was paired with a ninety-year-old golfer with perfect vision, who would be his spotter. On the first tee, the 80-year-old hit the ball. He asked his 90-year-old partner, "Where did it go?" After a moment, his ninety-year-old partner replied, "I can't remember."

Many people won't believe what they can't see. Jesus calls us to faith in Him, though we have not yet seen Him. One day soon, our faith will be made sight. Until that time, we have God's Word and the Holy Spirit to help us rejoice in things we can't yet see.

Lord Jesus, though I don't yet see You, I rejoice in Your work all around me. Until I am in Your presence, give me grace to live by faith and not by sight. I don't see You, but I love You. I am waiting for the day when I'll see You face to face.

WEDNESDAY

For he satisfies the longing soul,
and the hungry soul he fills with good things.
Psalm 107:9

Agreat tool to sooth babies is a pacifier. A pacifier is fake food – a piece of rubber designed to trick the child. Eventually, the baby catches on when his hunger isn't satisfied, and he's not going to be shy about letting you know he wants the real thing!

We all have a deep spiritual hunger that can only be satisfied by a relationship with Jesus Christ. The pacifiers of money, sex, achievement, education, and other things only satisfy us temporarily. Don't live your life being pacified by things that don't truly satisfy your real hunger. Instead, go to Jesus to satisfy the deepest longings of your heart.

––––––––––––

Lord Jesus, Your table is overflowing with good things that will satisfy my hungry soul. Help me to not fill up on junk, but to feast on all that You provide that will satisfy my deepest longings.

Thursday

The lines have fallen for me in pleasant places;
indeed, I have a beautiful inheritance.

Psalm 16:6

A skillful gardener knows how to make her plants flourish. She creates the borders, plants complementary flowers, protects her plants from weeds, and ensures the right amounts of water and fertilizer, all for her garden to grow beautifully.

David's life included its share of suffering. Yet, he described his life the way we might describe a garden: "pleasant" and "delightful." David knew God's sovereignty had made his life that way. Because God is sovereign, He has the power to do whatever He desires in your life. God is unfailingly good, you can trust that His plans are always the absolute best plans.

God, in Jesus Christ I have the beautiful inheritance of eternal life with You. Thank You that my trials are temporary and cannot compare to the glorious future that You are preparing for me.

FRIDAY

You keep him in perfect peace whose mind is stayed
on you, because he trusts in you.
Isaiah 26:3

The world is turbulent, and peace can be hard to find. Yet, God promises perfect peace when you trust in Him. The familiar Hebrew word for peace is *shalom.* The phrase translated *perfect peace* is actually simply *shalom, shalom.* When troubles multiply, so does God's peace.

Worries about the future are like a bundle of sticks too heavy for you to lift. God doesn't ask you to carry the whole load at once. He will untie the bundle, give you one small stick for today, and then help you carry it. Don't be weighed down by your cares. Trust in the Lord. He will give you complete peace.

Lord, help me to set my mind on You and trust You every day.
Then as worries try to move in, help me to close the door on
them with Your truth and keep them at bay by trusting You.

SATURDAY

In all things I have shown you that by working hard in this way we must help the weak and remember the words of the Lord Jesus, how he himself said, "It is more blessed to give than to receive."

Acts 20:35

Springs continually spill out their cold, clear water from below the surface to create beautiful rivers and streams. However, a pond just a block away can quickly become an eyesore! The pond continually receives water, but because it has no outlet, it can become stagnant and ugly. To be refreshing, water can't stand still; it needs to give itself away!

God created us to give. He blesses us when we give. Are you as eager to do things for others as you are to receive good things from them? Some of God's gracious blessings require no real effort from us. We simply open our hands and receive. The blessing of giving requires taking initiative. You can only experience the blessing of giving through the act of giving.

Lord Jesus, You are generous and giving to all. Help me to be like You, generously giving to others. Help me to always give in Your name, so that You receive the glory.

SUNDAY

Now we have received not the spirit of the world, but the Spirit who is from God, that we might understand the things freely given us by God.

1 Corinthians 2:12

My mom and dad recently purchased a new SUV. When they picked it up, their salesman spent over two hours showing them all the features, until they understood how to ring every bell and blow every whistle. The salesman wasn't trying to sell something new. He was showing them what they already had.

God's Holy Spirit lives in every believer. One of His roles is to show us the blessings we already have in Christ — His wisdom, His peace, and the truth of His Word. Today, praise God for the guidance of the Holy Spirit as you live for Jesus.

Father, Thank You for Your Holy Spirit living in me. Thank You that He teaches me Your Word as I read and study it. I surrender to Your leading through Your Spirit so that I can please You today.

MONDAY

*Now I would remind you, brothers, of the gospel
I preached to you, which you received, in which
you stand, and by which you are being saved,
if you hold fast to the word I preached to you—
unless you believed in vain.*

1 Corinthians 15:1-2

A s a teenager, I worked for a man who said, "That's the gospel!" in response to anything he agreed with. For instance, if someone said, "That's a delicious hamburger," he answered, "That's the gospel!" For him, *gospel* was simply a positive term with no clear meaning. Sadly, some use the word gospel in a similar way today.

The Bible says that the Gospel is this: Jesus Christ died for our sins, He was buried, and He rose from the grave on the third day so that we could have eternal life. The Gospel alone has the power to save everyone who will believe. The Gospel is God's greatest message.

---

*Lord God, Thank You for the simple Gospel of Jesus Christ.
Thank You that I am saved by believing Your message. Help me
to share Your message with others so they can be saved.*

TUESDAY

Then they cried to the Lord in their trouble, and he delivered them from their distress. He led them by a straight way till they reached a city to dwell in.
Psalm 107:6–7

A restless little boy tossed and turned in his bed. Eventually he called out, "Mom!" His mother got up from her bed and came to her son's room. "Mom, I can't sleep! I've tried everything!" "Well, come with me," she said. Together they went to the sofa where she held her restless son until he finally drifted into a peaceful sleep.

During the Babylonian exile, Israel found themselves in distressing places. So, what did God's people do? They called out to God for relief, and He answered and brought them to a place of protection. He brought them to Himself. Augustine said, "You have made us for yourself, and our hearts are restless until they rest in you." We will all wind up empty in our search for fulfillment until we come to Jesus Christ. Call on Him in your trouble, and you'll be satisfied.

Lord, Thank You for hearing my cries for help when I am in distress. When I'm in trouble, help me to first call out to You, and to enjoy the peace You give me.

WEDNESDAY

And rend your hearts and not your garments.
Return to the LORD your God, for he is gracious
and merciful, slow to anger, and abounding in
steadfast love; and he relents over disaster.

Joel 2:13

On my way out of a restaurant where I had just eaten, I took from a dish a mint wrapped in plastic. As I pulled opened the wrapper, I saw a message printed there. It said, "If you have ever had a meal this good before, then welcome back!" That was a bold claim. They were saying there's nothing this good anywhere else.

Nowhere else will you find life as good as it is with Jesus. His mercy, grace, forgiveness, and love are unsurpassed. When you go in the wrong direction, God calls you to turn around, and return to Him. That's repentance. And, when we return to Him, our Lord always says, "Welcome back!"

Lord God, I know that when I fail in my struggle with sin, You remain faithful and always call me to repent and return to You. Thank You that You never tire of forgiving my sin.

Thursday

And hope does not put us to shame, because
God's love has been poured into our hearts through
the Holy Spirit who has been given to us.
Romans 5:5

Remember the story of the Wizard of Oz? Dorothy, her dog Toto, and their friends travel to the Emerald City on the yellow brick road, hoping the wonderful Wizard of Oz will give the Lion courage, the Tin Man a heart, the Scarecrow a brain, and get Dorothy back home. When they finally meet the Wizard, they find he's just an ordinary man pulling a few strings. What a disappointment for the hopeful group!

When we put our hopes in people or things, we will ultimately be disappointed. But God never disappoints. He cares deeply for us, and His Holy Spirit fills our heart with His love.

God, Your steadfast love and the hope I have in Jesus Christ
are greater than my deepest disappointments. I praise You that
disappointment will not last forever, but Your love will.

FRIDAY

*He has delivered us from the domain of darkness
and transferred us to the kingdom of his beloved Son.*
Colossians 1:13

Delivery has become a way of life. Hardly a day goes by when I don't see the Amazon van, the FedEx truck, or the brown UPS van rolling through my neighborhood to make deliveries. Delivery seems to make the world go round!

God specializes in delivery! Through Jesus Christ, He delivers us from the kingdom of darkness to the kingdom of His beloved Son, Jesus Christ. Have you been delivered from darkness to God's kingdom? God wants to deliver you – not next day delivery, or two-day delivery, but right now when you repent of your sin and call on Jesus Christ to save you.

Father, how I thank You for Jesus! I turn from my sin and surrender to Jesus as my king. Please move me out of darkness into Your light. I want to be part of Your kingdom.

Saturday

Bondservants, obey your earthly masters with fear and trembling, with a sincere heart, as you would Christ.

Ephesians 6:5

The average American will work 90,000 hours in a lifetime. That's ten hours a day, seven days a week. No vacation and no days off for twenty-five years. I'm exhausted just thinking about it.

God made us to work. He cares about our work. God instructs us to obey our earthly masters. So if your boss tells you to do something, do it with respect and sincerity, unless it's against God's law, illegal, immoral, or unethical. Are you respectful of your boss and others in authority over you? Commit to do your work with sincerity, as unto Jesus, and not as unto men. Today when you go to work, remember: Jesus is your boss.

———————————

Father, Jesus is my Lord and master. You have ordained that I also have earthly masters. Help me to serve them today with a good heart, so that I please You above all.

SUNDAY

Masters, do the same to them, and stop your threatening, knowing that he who is both their Master and yours is in heaven, and that there is no partiality with him.

Ephesians 6:9

Everyone is a boss of someone. Even if you don't run a company, or manage people, every time you step up to a fast-food counter, for just a brief moment, the server works for you. That makes you the boss.

God requires that we treat our employees with fairness, patience, generosity, and kindness. As a manager, a boss, or even as a restaurant patron, you have a platform from which you can show Jesus to those who are watching. You have a boss in Heaven, so treat your employees with the same kindness He shows you!

Father, help me to be kind and compassionate to those who answer to me, always mindful that I answer to You for my words to them. Help me to treat others as You treat me.

MONDAY

Brothers, I do not consider that I have made it my own. But one thing I do: forgetting what lies behind and straining forward to what lies ahead, I press on toward the goal for the prize of the upward call of God in Christ Jesus.

Philippians 3:13-14

A man worried about his memory saw his doctor. His doctor said, "Well, we can't help your memory without harming your sight. Which do you want most: to see, or to remember?" The man answered, "I'd rather see where I'm going than remember where I've been!"

Focusing on past failures and sins keeps you from trusting God now. If you've repented of your sins and been forgiven, then leave the past where it belongs – in the past. Keep moving ahead to what God has for you. God doesn't dwell on your past; why should you?

God, it is such a relief that You don't remember my sins that I have confessed and forsaken. Help me to leave my past in the past, where You say it belongs because of the blood of Jesus Christ.

TUESDAY

Sanctify them in the truth; your Word is truth.
John 17:17

Perhaps the greatest battle in our culture today is over truth. Americans are skeptical about truthfulness in the media. Politicians and other influencers redefine terms to mislead us about what they really stand for. This lack of truth trickles down to every level. Seventy-one percent of high school students admit to cheating on an exam in the last twelve months. One third of adults say truth is always relative to the situation.

God's Word is truth. It is the standard by which we measure everything else. God's Word is the lens through which we measure every idea and action. Fill your mind with God's truth. It will sanctify you, making you more like Jesus, who Himself is the Truth.

Lord Jesus, help me to hold up every idea to the light of Your Word. Then help me to reject all that the world says is true but doesn't line up with Your truth. Your Word is truth.

WEDNESDAY

We love because he first loved us.
1 John 4:19

A little girl's bed was covered with her stuffed animals. One day, her mother walked past her room and saw her little girl in the middle of her bed, surrounded by her stuffed animals. She was holding one of them tightly and sobbing. Her mom said, "Honey, what's wrong?" And she said, "I hug them all the time; but they never hug me back."

God loves us so much, yet we often don't love Him back. He is so good to us. He gives us life. He provides for us and blesses our lives. He gave His own Son to die for us. Do you love God for all that He's done for you? His goodness should always draw us to love Him.

Father, Your amazing love caused You to forgive all my sin through Your Son, Jesus Christ. You give me good things every day. Your Spirit lives in me. I love You, Lord. Thank You for Your love.

Thursday

But I am not ashamed, for I know whom I have believed, and I am convinced that he is able to guard until that day what has been entrusted to me.

2 Timothy 1:12

Reach back in your memory to when you first got to know your closest friends or your spouse. It was a process, wasn't it? Revealing your thoughts to them. Letting them share their thoughts with you. Eventually, you come to know the people closest to you. And once you really knew them, you trusted them.

The same holds in our relationship with God. The more we know Him through prayer and His Word, the more we learn His thoughts and character, the more we see how He's worked in the past, the more deeply we can trust Him to keep His promises for our future.

Lord Jesus, Thank You for my relationship with You. Thank You for daily opportunities to learn to trust You. Thank You for building a history of Your faithfulness to me. You are trustworthy.

FRIDAY

*Oh, the depth of the riches and wisdom and
knowledge of God! How unsearchable are his
judgments and how inscrutable his ways!*
Romans 11:33

There are hundreds of thousands of English words available to us to use to communicate. Most people know about twenty to thirty-five thousand words. Even if you know fewer than ten percent of the words that are available to you, there are still multiple ways to say what you mean. In the English-speaking world, we have lots of options!

In almost any language, the first word of the above verse is the same: Oh. It's an exclamation that is difficult, even impossible to define, though we know deep down what it means – God's riches, wisdom, knowledge, judgments, and ways are deeper than words can express. No words can fully express the depth of who God is. His awesomeness is greater than anything we can conceive or articulate!

---

*Oh God, I can never adequately express how awesome You are,
or how grateful I am for Your salvation. Today I simply say
thank You, God, for who You are, and thank You for saving me.*

SATURDAY

Therefore be imitators of God, as beloved children.
Ephesians 5:1

When my wife Michele and I were dating, she called our house one day and my dad answered the phone. Apparently I sounded just like him, because she talked to him a couple of minutes before she realized she was talking to my father and not to me! She's still embarrassed when she thinks about it.

The Bible says that we are to be like our heavenly Father. We can look like Him when we live holy, generous lives, avoiding immorality, impurity, and greed. We sound like Him when we extend kindness and forgiveness to those who hurt us. In fact, you'll never look more like your Heavenly Father than when you forgive those who He forgives.

Father, help my words to be Your words and empower me to forgive those who hurt or offend me. I want to be like You – gracious, compassionate, and generous. Help me be holy as You are holy.

SUNDAY

Forever, O LORD, your word is
firmly fixed in the heavens.
Psalm 119:89

One of my favorite pastors used to ask, "Has it ever oc-curred to you that nothing has ever occurred to God?" That means that God never claps His palm to his forehead and says, "I never thought of that before."

God's knowledge is perfect. God's Word is not some-thing that God made up as He went along. From eterni-ty, He has understood and foreseen exactly how things are going to pan out. As a result, His Word stands firm in the heavens, unchanging and perfect. It was always there, eter-nal, in His mind. For that reason, God can be absolutely trusted. He is never caught off-guard and never surprised.

———————

Lord, Your Word is true and as sound today as in the time it
was written down. You will never change; You are forever holy
and perfect. I trust You to guide me through Your Word.

MONDAY

*For I have given you an example, that you
also should do just as I have done to you.*
John 13:15

Remember learning to tie your shoes? Your mom might have said, "Cross the laces, then put one under the other and pull. Now, make a loop with the lace on the left. Then take the lace in your right hand and…" Well, that wouldn't have worked for me. I needed my mom to say, "Here, let me show you."

To learn how to please God, we can simply open our Bibles to see how Jesus lived, and then do what He did, because He came to earth to say, "Here, let me show you." Learning how to please God isn't a mystery. Jesus came to show us how.

---

*Lord Jesus, help me to live as You taught Your disciples,
obeying all that You say. Help me also to teach others
to follow You, making disciples as You commanded.*

TUESDAY

And you, who were dead in your trespasses and the uncircumcision of your flesh, God made alive together with him, having forgiven us all our trespasses.
Colossians 2:13

Just one word can make a big difference. For example, listen to this sentence: "I mowed my lawn *only* yesterday." Move the word *only,* and it says, "I mowed *only* my lawn yesterday." Move the word *only* again, and it says, "I *only* mowed my lawn yesterday." One word makes a big difference.

One word makes all the difference in your standing with God. That word is *forgiven.* We deserve God's wrath for every sin we commit. But everyone who trusts in Jesus Christ has forgiveness of every sin – past, present, and future.

Holy God, I was dead in my sins before You saved me. I praise You that Jesus' death on the cross paid for my sin, and that now I have everlasting life through Jesus Christ! What a great gift!

Wednesday

If you then are not able to do the least,
why are you anxious for the rest?
Luke 12:26

One of the frustrating truths in life is that weeds will grow absolutely anywhere – and especially where they're not wanted. But one day while examining my yard, I noticed that where there was thick, healthy grass, there was no room for weeds to grow. The healthy grass crowded them out.

Worry is a weed in our hearts and minds, taking over where there is little faith. When your life is filled with trust in God, worries will be crowded out. Every day, sow seeds of faith in God and His promises. Healthy, growing faith will choke worry out of your life.

———————————

Lord Jesus, my life will always be full of things over which
I have no control. Today, instead of worrying, I will trust You.
Please give me Your grace to not be anxious.

Thursday

And whatever you ask in prayer,
you will receive, if you have faith.
Matthew 21:22

Did you know that cement will never become concrete until you add water? A bag of powdery cement can sit on the shelf for years and years, but without adding water, it will never become rock solid.

Right now, God has the power to do anything and everything in your life! His power is available to you, but His power only takes effect in your life when you add faith. God wants to do great things in your life! Nothing is impossible for Him. But we need to ask God to give us faith to fully trust Him. And when we do, He can do something incredible, something real, and something concrete in your life today.

Father, Thank You for the gift of prayer. As I bring my needs to You, as well as my praise and thanks, help my faith to grow as I trust You to provide all I need at the right time.

FRIDAY

*Praise him for his mighty deeds; praise him
according to his excellent greatness!*
Psalm 150:2

A pastor was talking to a six-year-old boy. He said, "So your mother prays for you each night. That's wonderful. What does she say?" The little boy said, "She prays, 'Praise God; he's in bed.'" Well, there's always something to praise Him for.

Think about the many things that God has done for you. He created you; he sustains you every day of your life. He protects you. He has redeemed you by the blood of His very own Son, Jesus Christ. Every day of your life, God does great and mighty things for you. And if you open your eyes, you can see them. There is always, always a reason to praise God!

God, You always deserve my praise! My life is full of Your blessings. Help me to keep praise on my lips today as I remember Your salvation and the good things You have done for me.

SATURDAY

*Keep your life free from love of money, and be
content with what you have, for he has said,
"I will never leave you nor forsake you."*
Hebrews 13:5

A wealthy man saw a fisherman sitting lazily beside his
boat. He went down and asked, "Why aren't you out
there fishing? If you catch more fish than you need, you
could earn more money and buy a better boat and catch
even more fish. You could purchase nylon nets, catch more
fish, and make even more money. Soon you would be rich
like me, and you could sit down and enjoy life!" The fisherman replied, "What do you think I'm doing now?"

We live in a never-enough world. But regardless of
whether we have much or little, we can be content because
we have the love of God. He will never forsake us, and in
him we have all that we need.

---

*Father, my contentment relies on my relationship with You,
and not on how much stuff I have. Lord, help me to find
my satisfaction in You rather than in accumulating more.*

SUNDAY

*For we are his workmanship, created in Christ
Jesus for good works, which God prepared
beforehand, that we should walk in them.*

Ephesians 2:10

When I was in high school, I worked at a building
supply store with an older retired man named
Frank. Though Frank was a rough, tough and abrupt man,
he would still call his wife during every shift. Each day I listened to him talk to his wife with sweet and tender words.
One day I asked one of our co-workers, "What's Frank's
wife's name?" He answered, "Well, I think her name is
'Beautiful.'" That was the only name we had ever heard
Frank call her.

When God looks at you, he says, "beautiful," because
we are His masterpiece. We can do nothing to make ourselves beautiful to God. Because Jesus cleanses us from sin,
and gives us His robes of righteousness, we truly are beautiful to God.

---

*God, thank You for setting Your love on me and for saving me for
a good purpose: to serve You and let Your glory shine through me.
I praise You for making me beautiful for Your glory.*

MONDAY

But the day of the Lord will come like a thief, and then the heavens will pass away with a roar, and the heavenly bodies will be burned up and dissolved, and the earth and the works that are done on it will be exposed.

2 Peter 3:10

I heard a story of a man named John who was in San Diego during the spread of wildfires. One night he was awakened by his dogs barking at the first spark that had spread to his front yard. John and another man began driving throughout their area honking and yelling for people to evacuate. The next day, John and the firefighters were saddened to see that because some people spent too much time packing their things, they didn't make it out in time.

The Bible clearly warns us to be prepared for the day Jesus Christ will return. The day of the Lord is not unexpected, so be ready! Share the gospel with those in danger of being without Jesus on that day. Today is the day of salvation; don't wait! Jesus is coming back.

Lord, I don't want to be caught unprepared for Your return. Help me to serve You each day with a pure heart so that when Jesus Christ appears, I will be ready and not ashamed.

TUESDAY

On that day, when evening had come, he said to them, "Let us go across to the other side." And leaving the crowd, they took him with them in the boat, just as he was. And other boats were with him.
Mark 4:35–36

When I lived in Florida, I learned that an approaching hurricane will keep you on your toes. We tried to prepare by watching the spaghetti models. But there's no type of pasta that's going to accurately predict where a hurricane will end up.

As you sail upon the tumultuous seas of life, you can successfully survive any storm by doing this one thing: make sure that Jesus is in your boat. Jesus is more powerful than every storm in your life. Keep your eyes on Him and go where He goes. He will always keep you on course.

Lord Jesus, You do not intend for me to navigate this life by my own wits. Thank You for inviting me to join You, and for staying with me in stormy seas. I trust You to guard me always.

Wednesday

*Where shall I go from your Spirit or
where shall I flee from your presence?*
Psalm 139:7

Sports journalist Charlie Jones interviewed members of the United States rowing team at the 1996 Olympics. He asked questions like: What if it rains during the race? What if your oar breaks? What if the wind blows you off course? Every athlete offered the same answer to these questions: *That's outside my boat.* In other words, they didn't worry about things they couldn't control.

We have no control over storms in our lives. Jesus will not abandon ship when the storms come. He sails with you into every one of them. So make sure that Jesus is in your boat, and keep your eyes on Him. His presence in your life overrides your storm.

Father, You are sovereign over every moment of my life. Thank You that I am never out of Your presence. I praise You for Your faithful care for me and that You will never ever forsake me.

Thursday

And he awoke and rebuked the wind and said to the sea, "Peace! Be still!" And the wind ceased, and there was a great calm.

Mark 4:39

A man walking past a ballfield spotted the kid in right field. He was smiling and twirling around, doing what little kids do. "What inning is it?" the man asked the boy. "First," Said the boy. "What's the score?" asked the man. "They're beatin' us eighteen to nothin'," said the kid. ""Well son, why are you so happy?" The boy said, "Because we haven't had our first at-bat yet."

If you're in a stormy situation today, it doesn't matter what the score is. Jesus *always* wins, and His team always wins. So take courage; Jesus has the authority to bring peace and victory to your storm.

———————————

Lord Jesus, You are my peace. Thank You that whatever threatens my peace must bow to You. Lord, You have the power to calm my heart even when the storm rages. I will trust You today.

Friday

And they were filled with great fear and said to one another, "Who then is this, that even the wind and the sea obey him?"
Mark 4:41

In my office, I have a beautiful photo of a boat on the Sea of Galilee in a moment when the water is calm and peaceful. Hanging beside that photo is a copy of Rembrandt's painting of a boat on that same sea, where the disciples are huddled together, panic-stricken because of a great storm. But in that dark scene, a faint light shows Jesus, sleeping peacefully in the back of the boat. Unlike His friends, He isn't panicked at all.

Life is often frightening for us. But Jesus is more powerful than any storm that blows into your life. No matter how troubling, every storm that comes must obey Jesus. He's in charge, so don't you be afraid.

Lord Jesus, everything in all of creation must obey You, so I will entrust myself to You today. You are more powerful than anything that can hurt me. I praise You; You are God over all.

Saturday

*And behold, there arose a great storm on
the sea, so that the boat was being swamped
by the waves; but he was asleep.*
Matthew 8:24

If you receive bad news, and the bottom drops out of your life, you'll probably spend a good deal of worry on what's going to happen next. You'll ask questions like, "How hard will this storm be? What's going to happen next? Will I make it?" Those are natural questions.

But you can be confident that because Jesus has a purpose for you, He will not let you go until He's taken you where He intends for you to be. His purpose overrules your storm. Your storms always have to bend to Jesus' plan for your life. He will work all things, even your storm, for your good.

---

*Lord Jesus, because You are God, I know that I will come through
every storm safely. Thank You that You work even the worst
storms for my good and to accomplish Your purpose in my life.*

Sunday

For we know that if the tent that is our earthly home is destroyed, we have a building from God, a house not made with hands, eternal in the heavens.

2 Corinthians 5:1

A lady looking in the mirror spied several new wrinkles in her forehead. She was so upset that she went looking for her husband to complain. When she found him, she pointed toward her forehead and cried, "I can't believe I have these!" Her husband kissed her on the forehead and said, "Sweetheart, I love every one of those gray hairs." At least he tried.

Creaky knees, achy joints, and blurry eyes shout loudly that our bodies are wearing out. But when time is over and God makes all things new, He has a perfect resurrection body for His people! Even if everything hurts today, be encouraged; better days are ahead!

God, my aches and pains remind me that this body won't last forever. They also remind me that because of Jesus, one day I will rise with a sinless resurrected body! Thank You for eternal life!

MONDAY

Let everything that has breath
praise the LORD! Praise the LORD!
Psalm 150:6

Samuel Scull's farm was torn apart in an overnight storm. His roof was gone, the garden was destroyed. Dead chickens were strewn about the barnyard. But as morning dawned, Samuel saw a battered rooster climb out through the debris. Amazingly, that rooster, dripping wet and bedraggled, still flapped his bony wings and crowed to welcome the morning.

As long as we're breathing, we're commanded to praise the Lord. Even when it seems that your world has been blown away, when we trust God, He strengthens us to climb out of the rubble and to sing His praise. God hears and He blesses the praises of His people. So today, whatever you're going through, praise the Lord! God will bless you when you praise Him.

Lord, for as long as I live, I will have the only tools I need to praise You: breath and a voice! Help my life to be marked by praise to You in prayer, and to speak Your praise to others.

TUESDAY

*And thus Abraham, having patiently
waited, obtained the promise.*
Hebrews 6:15

The word *hope* is one we often use in negative ways. For instance, a student might say, "I didn't study for that test; I hope I passed!" Or a person undergoing medical tests might say, "I hope nothing bad is wrong with me." In both of those situations, the word *hope* communicates fear and uncertainty.

But in the Bible, *hope* is a word of faith and sureness. Our certain hope in Jesus Christ holds us securely in His presence – even when the days are stormy. The strength of our anchor is the completed work of Jesus Christ that gives you unrestricted access to God. Your hope in Jesus is certain, so be patient, and do not fear!

Lord Jesus, You are my hope, both for today and for the future. I want to be faithful like Abraham as I wait for Your promises to be fulfilled. Thank You that every promise of God is yes in You.

WEDNESDAY

My flesh and my heart may fail, but God is the strength of my heart and my portion forever.
Psalm 73:26

I heard about a basketball game that had an awful referee. The home team continually cheated, shoved, and fouled their opponents, but the whistle never blew. The referee even declined to award points to the other team. The game obviously was one-sided due to this referee, and as a result, the losing players were overwhelmingly weary.

The world sometimes treats us the same way. When nothing goes as planned, we keep losing, and we feel worn-out, we must look to God for strength. In the world, we will face tough and unrelenting opposition, but Jesus Christ gives us all the strength we need when we are weary.

———————————

Father God, when I am weary, strengthen me to live faithfully for You. When I am tired, help me to breathe prayers of praise and thanksgiving. You are more than enough for my hardest days.

Thursday

Nevertheless, I am continually with you;
you hold my right hand.
Psalm 73:23

There was a very ill man who went to see a doctor. After an examination the doctor told him "There's nothing wrong with you physically, but you look very weary." The doctor suggested that he go see the performance of Cervantes the Clown, thinking that a good laugh and a smile would help cure him. The ill man replied, "That won't work. I am Cervantes the clown."

It's difficult for us to tell others to trust in God when we personally have a difficult time doing so. This world can make us weary, but that's when we must lean on God the most. When the world is beating you down, remember that your God is continually with you.

Lord, no one is faithful like You. There is no other source of strength when the world is tough. Even when circumstances say otherwise, You are good and trustworthy. I trust You today.

Friday

Because he holds fast to me in love, I will deliver him;
I will protect him, because he knows my name.

Psalm 91:14

Howard Rutledge was an American Navy pilot whose plane was shot down in the Vietnam War. He was captured by the Vietnamese. For over seven years he survived in a cramped prison cell, fighting off filth, rats, and painful loneliness. It was in that prison that he turned to God. When Howard was finally released, he told everyone that though he was alone, he had experienced God's very real presence in that prison.

We can find God's blessing, even in the midst of terrible loneliness. When you feel the pain of being alone, God is still with you, even this very minute.

Father, give me Your grace to keep loving You when life is hard.
My feelings of loneliness don't mean that I am alone. You are
always with me, and You will deliver me at the right time.

SATURDAY

He will not let your foot be moved;
he who keeps you will not slumber.
Psalm 121:3

A t bedtime, when we turn off all of our distractions, worry can turn up the volume like a noisy neighbor and disturb our peace. Does worry keep you up at night? Or are you constantly thinking about the next thing that you have to do when morning finally comes?

Worrying can rob you of sleep and rest. The busyness of our lives can distract us from remembering that God is always watching over us, even while we sleep. Before you close your eyes tonight, thank God that He is with you. God has promised to watch over you and protect you, so you can rest and sleep, because, praise God, He never sleeps!

Father God, as I turn the light off to sleep tonight, remind me
that You are watching over me even when I don't realize it.
Thank You that You are a faithful guard over my life.

SUNDAY

We have this as a sure and steadfast anchor of the soul,
a hope that enters into the inner place behind the curtain.
Hebrews 6:19

The website for the Wayzata Nautical Gift Company shows a photo of a beautiful anchor they offer for sale. It's large, has two sturdy looking prongs, and a massive chain. It looks heavy, like it could dig firmly into the sea floor, but it won't. It doesn't go down to the bottom at all, because it's made of Styrofoam. It's just a prop.

We can find ourselves attempting to firmly anchor our lives by Styrofoam anchors – health, education, success, money, and friendships – but they won't hold us steady for long. There is only one true anchor for our souls, and that is our hope in Jesus Christ.

Father, Thank You that the hope I have in Jesus Christ holds me when even the smallest waves would set me adrift. I praise You that in Christ, I have hope that will not be moved for eternity.

Monday

*Looking to Jesus, the founder and perfecter
of our faith, who for the joy that was set before
him endured the cross, despising the shame, and
is seated at the right hand of the throne of God.*

Hebrews 12:2

A shepherd was herding about two thousand sheep across the plains. One night as darkness came, he made a fire in the open field for him to stay warm as he tended his flock. Suddenly there was an unmistakable wail of coyote calls. The shepherd hurried to toss another log onto the fire to bring additional light. As he heightened his watch of the flock, the shepherd saw the firelight reflected in the eyes of all those sheep. The sheep weren't looking out to the scary darkness; they were looking to their shepherd.

Jesus is the Good Shepherd. He is always with His people, watching over them to protect them from their enemies. Keep your eyes on Jesus; He is all you need when the night is dark and the enemy howls.

Lord Jesus, Thank You for the great price You paid on the cross to make me Your sheep. You endured the cross, so I know You will do everything else needed to keep me safe from the enemy.

TUESDAY

Everyone then who hears these words of
mine and does them will be like a wise man
who built his house on the rock.
Matthew 7:24

Standing on the beautiful Golden Gate Bridge can be unnerving, because you can feel that giant bridge sway slightly with wind, waves, and traffic. But right in the middle of that bridge is the safest place to be during an earthquake, because every piece of that bridge is somehow connected to cables that are anchored in bedrock beneath San Francisco Bay. That bridge won't fall when it's shaken, because it's securely anchored to the rock.

Standing with Jesus is the safest place you can be when your life is shaken. You may feel the sway, but you'll be absolutely secure with Jesus. Our hope in Christ is sure and steadfast for all of eternity.

Lord Jesus, I'm so thankful that even when I feel the sway
caused by difficult days, I am completely secure in You.
I can never be shaken because You will never fail.

WEDNESDAY

He restores my soul. He leads me in the
paths of righteousness for his name's sake.
Psalm 23:3

A little boy named Jarrod was trying to learn how to get home in case he ever got lost. His mom and dad made sure he learned his address and phone number. One night Jarrod and his dad were outside walking. "Jarrod, do you know where we are right now?" "No, Dad. I don't." His dad looked down at him and said, "Well then, it sounds like you might be lost." Jarrod replied, "No Dad, I can't be lost because I'm with you."

We can never be lost when we're walking with Jesus. When we learn to let God take us where He wants, He will always take us where we need to go. His paths are always good and right.

Lord God, Your way is always the right way. You will always do good for me because You are careful to protect the reputation of Your own name. I surrender to Your leading.

Thursday

The Lord is my Shepherd; I shall not want.
Psalm 23:1

I heard a story of a young girl who wanted to memorize the twenty-third psalm for her father. She read the passage over and over, and even practiced in front of a mirror. She wanted it to be perfect. She went to her father and said, "The Lord is my shepherd; that's all I want." Though she got the words wrong, that little girl got the truth right.

When we see Jesus as our Shepherd, He is all we will ever want! He is all we will ever need. In every time, in every season, and in every situation, Jesus is right beside you. Look to the Lord God today, for He truly is your Shepherd.

———————

Lord, You are my Good Shepherd. You faithfully care for me so that there is nothing that I really need that I do not have. Thank You for making me Your sheep; I would be lost without You.

FRIDAY

Trust in him at all times, O people; pour out your heart before him; God is a refuge for us.
Psalm 62:8

In 1864, when the Civil War was raging, it became common practice to put the words *In God We Trust* on US coins. In 1865, Abraham Lincoln signed into law that every coin minted by the US would have those four words: *In God We Trust.* In 1956, our country adopted those simple words as our national motto: *In God We Trust.*

What do those four words mean? They must be more than just words. They must be more than just a sentiment or motto. God calls us to trust in Him. And when we truly live our lives day by day saying, "In God we trust," it transforms every part of our lives.

Lord God, there is much in the world that I'd like to hide from. But I trust in you, O God. You are the refuge of my life.

SATURDAY

He only is my rock and my salvation,
my fortress; I shall not be shaken.
Psalm 62:6

One evening as a grandfather was playing games with his beloved grandsons, there was an unexpected knock at the door. Startled, the grandfather got up to see who was there. Instantly, he felt one of his grandsons close to his side and holding tightly to his hand. He opened the door to a family friend. "Grandaddy, is everything okay?" "Of course, son, there is nothing to worry about." The boy immediately relaxed. Later on, that grandfather realized, "My grandson's courage came from the one he was clinging to."

We can place our whole lives in the hand of our heavenly Father. Cling tightly to Jesus; in Him you will find strength and protection.

———————

God, no enemy can harm me because I am in You. Jesus has saved me, and He is the rock upon which I build my life. I will love You and trust You today because nothing can shake Jesus.

SUNDAY

And these words that I command you today shall be on your heart. You shall teach them diligently to your children, and shall talk of them when you sit in your house, and when you walk by the way, and when you lie down, and when you rise.

Deuteronomy 6:6–7

To make sure every generation remembered, the people of Israel were to talk about God's commandments constantly. Even what they wore and how they decorated their houses were to serve as reminders of God's law.

How well are you doing in teaching your children and grandchildren the importance of obeying God? In ancient Israel, children usually spent countless hours with their parents. They had many opportunities to pass on the blessings of the covenant to the next generation. Especially in our fragmented culture, with so many demands pulling on us and our kids, let's diligently take every opportunity to teach our children who God is and how to obey Him.

Lord God, no matter how I've done in the past, from this day on, help me to take every opportunity to teach my children and grandchildren about You. I want them to follow Jesus.

Monday

*And the Lord came and stood, calling as at
other times, "Samuel! Samuel!" And Samuel said,
"Speak, for your servant hears."*
1 Samuel 3:10

O ne rule of being a good leader is to avoid surrounding
yourself with yes-men who will support every idea
you have, whether good or bad. You can run off the rails
and crash without someone at your side who's willing to
help you recognize your bad decisions, even those made
with the best of intentions.

When decisions loom, we ask God to speak. But what
we sometimes want to hear is His approval of our decisions
already made. God's ways are higher than our ways. His
will for you may not conform to your plans. Always listen
to God with a pure heart, willing to obey all what He says.

---

*Lord, thank you for speaking to me through your Word
and in prayer. Help me to truly desire to follow your ways
and not my own.*

Tuesday

And this is the promise that he
made to us—eternal life.
1 John 2:25

We make all kinds of promises, but sometimes we either don't or can't keep them. Sometimes we forget. Sometimes we make promises that we don't intend to keep. Sometimes we make foolish promises we can't possibly keep, or our circumstances frustrate our plans to keep our promises.

But God never, ever breaks a promise. Nothing ever slips His mind, so He cannot forget. He cannot lie, so He cannot make promises He doesn't intend to keep. He is all powerful, so nothing can prevent Him from being able to keep His promises. God will keep every promise He has made in His Word. So obey Him, and wait patiently. Not one of His promises will fail.

Lord Jesus, I know that Your promises are sure and that
I can count on You to keep them all. You are faithful,
so I will trust You today.

WEDNESDAY

He who believes in me, as the Scripture has said,
out of his heart will flow rivers of living water.
John 7:38

The greatest danger to any ancient city during a siege was never the enemy outside the walls. When an army attacked a city like Jerusalem, they simply surrounded the city and waited for the food and water to run out. When the city ran out of resources, it could be taken almost without a fight.

Jesus said the Holy Spirit is God's living water, and this water flows not as a trickle, but as a river! With God's Spirit living inside you, you can outlast any attack from your spiritual enemy, the devil. God's Holy Spirit is your unending source of life.

Lord Jesus, Thank You that the Holy Spirit is a continual source of strength and comfort in my life. Today, I will depend on the power of Your Spirit to fill me to live for You.

THURSDAY

For my people have committed two evils:
they have forsaken me, the fountain of living waters,
and hewed out cisterns for themselves,
broken cisterns that can hold no water.

Jeremiah 2:13

He arrived at the plant and within minutes he found the problem. So he took his sketch of the machine and drew a red X over the part that needed repair, including a note that said, "Fix this."

When the company received the bill for his services, they demanded an explanation for his charge of $10,000. He responded: "For inspecting the equipment and drawing an X, $1. For knowing where to draw the X, $9,999."

God knows exactly what causes our lives to be broken. He knows where to put the X. So if your life needs fixing, ask God to show you what needs attention. He will help you make the repairs when you determine to do all that He shows you.

Lord, I ask Your Holy Spirit to put His finger on the area of my life that needs attention. Help me to make that part of my life right and pleasing to You. Thank You for Your grace and mercy.

Friday

The grass withers, the flower fades,
but the word of our God will stand forever.
Isaiah 40:8

One day as I was cleaning out books in my library, I came across some manuals that came with a computer that I bought several years ago. Do you know how much those books are worth today? Nothing. Hundreds of pages of information that was once important are now irrelevant, because all of the knowledge of man is passing away.

Man's word is faulty. Man's word is fading. If you're relying on the words of men, you will find them to be unreliable, capricious, uncertain, and passing away. You can count on God's Word. His Word is firm, and His Word is faithful. We can give God thanks for that today!

God, Your Word will never be outdated. It is always perfect, and it is the lens through which I need to evaluate everything in my world. Thank You for the power of Your Word to change me.

SATURDAY

On the day I called, you answered me;
my strength of soul you increased.
Psalm 138:3

When we ask God for the desires of our hearts, we're often disappointed when He answers "no." Ruth Graham, Billy Graham's wife, said this: "God hasn't always answered 'yes' to my prayers. If He had, I would have married the wrong man, several times."

God isn't like a genie in a bottle, who grants your wishes even if they would hurt you. We sometimes ask God for foolish things - we just don't know it at the time!

God always answers our prayers, and sometimes His answer is no. When we're in heaven, we'll see that God's *nos* were His most loving answers to some of our most desirous prayers.

Heavenly Father, Thank You for saying no to my foolish requests. I praise You that Your answers to my prayers are always loving and truly best for me. I trust Your answers, even Your nos.

Sunday

Beware of false prophets, who come to you in sheep's clothing but inwardly are ravenous wolves.
Matthew 7:15

A sinister wolf dressed himself in the fleece of a sheep and grazed with a flock unnoticed. At the end of the day, when the sheep were secured inside the pen, the wolf began to stalk his next meal. But the shepherd returned unexpectedly and saw the wolf taking aim at his sheep. The shepherd killed the wolf immediately.

Teachers of false doctrine are wolves in sheep's clothing. Their intention is to destroy God's flock. Every preacher and every Bible teacher must line up with only one standard: God's Word.

It's imperative to know God's Word so that you can recognize false teaching. Any teaching that deviates even slightly from the Bible must be rejected.

Lord, give me discernment to recognize false teachers. Help me to study and know Your Word so that I am not taken in by wolves dressed like sheep. Lord, protect my church from false teachers.

MONDAY

They encircle me with words of hate
and attack me without cause.

Psalm 109:3

It's a story I see repeated on the news all too often. A driver in the lane he's supposed to be in suddenly encounters a vehicle speeding toward him in the wrong lane. Generally, the story only makes the news because someone has been hurt or killed. These days, even staying in your lane is dangerous.

Don't be surprised when you encounter opposition for serving Jesus Christ. Satan is always opposed to God's work. He will send danger careening into your lane as you seek to obey Jesus Christ, especially when you are working for the sake of the gospel. Opposition may mean you are definitely doing something right, so trust the Lord to keep you safe, and continue in your lane.

Lord God, these are trying days when the wicked spew words of hate against Your people. Strengthen me Lord, and help me to stand firmly for Jesus, even when I'm attacked for doing so.

Tuesday

Jesus looked up and saw the rich putting their gifts into the offering box. And he saw a poor widow put in two small copper coins.

Luke 21:1-2

One day I saw a penny and a dime on the ground. I hardly gave them a thought. What if I had picked them up and made them my offering to the Lord the next Sunday? I can safely say that Jesus would not have been impressed.

But the poor widow's tiny offering gave Jesus joy! He knew well the sacrifice she was making. Sacrificial giving brings joy to Jesus. He doesn't focus on the size of your gift, but on what you have remaining. Let's be sacrificial givers; it will give Jesus joy, and you'll have joy, as well!

———————

Jesus, Thank You for the joy of sacrificial giving. Help me to count Your kingdom as more valuable than my money and possessions, and give generously and cheerfully to You.

WEDNESDAY

*For God so loved the world, that he gave his
only Son, that whoever believes in him should
not perish but have eternal life.*
John 3:16

Several years ago a parachute instructor, Michael Costello, jumped out of an airplane with a novice sky diver named Gareth Griffith. Tragically, their parachute failed. Just before hitting the ground, Costello rolled over so that he would hit the ground first and Griffith would land on top of him. Costello died instantly, but Griffith survived. Costello died willingly to save Griffith's life.

Because of sin, we are fallen, separated from God, and deserving of God's judgment. Jesus willingly took the brunt of God's judgment when He died on the cross in our place. Jesus loves you and died to save your life for eternity. Trust Him and be saved today!

God, You showed the greatest love of all when You gave Your Son Jesus to die on the cross for sinners. I trust Jesus as my Savior. Help me to share that love with others so they can be saved.

341

THURSDAY

*As for you, you meant evil against me, but God
meant it for good, to bring it about that many
people should be kept alive, as they are today.*

Genesis 50:20

Perhaps you would call your life or your family dysfunc-
tional. Joseph's family was the definition of messed up!
His dad Jacob had children by four women. His siblings hated him. They trafficked him, selling him into slavery in a foreign country. He was imprisoned for years on a false charge
of attempted rape. He had plenty of reasons to be bitter and
vengeful, but instead, he remained faithful and forgiving.

Through all the years of hatred, jealousy, and abuse he
suffered, Joseph continually entrusted himself to God. And
God used everything that others had meant to hurt Joseph
for good, to save and preserve his family. You, too, can trust
God when people intend to hurt you. Be patient; God *will*
bring good out of your pain.

---

*God, thank You for Your power to use terrible situations for good
in my life. I don't know what good You're working in my current
difficulties, but I trust You to do great things through them.*

Friday

They go from strength to strength;
each one appears before God in Zion.
Psalm 84:7

If you're going on a long journey, you start out the first day fresh and ready to go. Every hundred miles or so of driving, you get a little more tired, and a little more weary. By the time you reach your destination, you're exhausted. No wonder my dad was always irritable on our first day of vacation!

In our own power we move along from strength to weariness. But when we rely on the Lord, He increases our strength. The closer you get to the Lord, the stronger you become, because you don't operate in your power, but in His. So rely on the Lord when you are weary. He will always provide strength for today, and bright hope for tomorrow!

Lord, Thank You for Your promise that one day I will be in Your presence forever. For now, I'm relying on You to strengthen me moment by moment. Thank You for giving me what I need today.

Saturday

For the LORD God is a sun and shield; the LORD bestows favor and honor. No good thing does he withhold from those who walk uprightly.

Psalm 84:11

People dream of winning the lottery. They think, "If I had millions of dollars, my troubles would be over!" Statistics tell us that seventy percent of lottery winners are broke five years after winning. Why? They don't have that money; that money has them. What they think would be a good thing becomes a terrible burden.

So many times the shiny, beautiful things that the world offers, things we think would be really good, wind up being rotten. God has promised to give us only good things. Everything God gives us is good. If He withholds something, it's because it would be bad for us. When God withholds something you long for, He's protecting you. You can trust Him.

Lord, so many things appeal to my flesh, but You know that they would be harmful to me. Help me to trust Your protection when You withhold those things from me.

SUNDAY

For the eyes of the LORD run to and fro throughout the whole earth, to give strong support to those whose heart is blameless toward him. You have done foolishly in this, for from now on you will have wars.

2 Chronicles 16:9

A convicted criminal was eulogizing his deceased gang leader. He said, "People say pretty mean things about Harry. It's true – Harry was a thief, a cheat, a liar, and a terrorist." And then he said this: "But man, Harry could really sing!"

Sometimes we try to cover our own wickedness by amplifying what we get right. It might sound like this: "Well, yes, I'm lazy. I'm selfish. And I have a bad temper. But I teach Sunday School!" Or, "I sing in the choir!" God strongly supports those daily whose walk is consistently holy and righteous. That's what it means to live a blameless life, and to be a man or woman after God's own heart.

O Lord, I am a sinner and can only do anything good by Your grace. But Lord, I want to be holy like You. Make my desire to be blameless before You and help me to strive for holiness in my life.

MONDAY

*For we all stumble in many ways. And if anyone
does not stumble in what he says, he is a perfect
man, able also to bridle his whole body.*

James 3:2

A company that manufactured earth-moving equipment made one machine called the Model G. A salesman was asked one day what the G stood for. The salesman, pretty quick on the trigger, answered almost instantly, "Well, I guess that G stands for gossip, because this machine moves a lot of dirt really fast."

God's people are called to put away unholy speech; that includes gossip. Don't get drawn into a dirt-moving conversation with others. Don't be part of the rumor mill. Don't share confidential information about others as prayer requests. A man or woman of God doesn't engage in gossip. Don't let your tongue run wild! Be careful to keep your words under control.

---

*Lord Jesus, help me to judge rightly what conversations I don't
need to be part of! Help me today to keep my tongue under the
control of Your Spirit so that all of my words please You.*

TUESDAY

*He has told you, O man, what is good; and what
does the LORD require of you but to do justice, and to
love kindness, and to walk humbly with your God?*
Micah 6:8

Columnist Dave Barry is known for his humor. He may
have been dead serious when he said this: "If someone
is nice to you, but rude to the waiter, they are not a nice
person." That's a great rule to measure your friends by. It's a
great rule to measure yourself by!

True character is revealed in how you treat people you
perceive as lower in status than you. Kindness, or the lack
of it, is an accurate measure of your relationship with Jesus Christ, because kindness is evidence of the Holy Spirit's
work in your life. God is kind to you. So honor God by
paying it forward. God's people are to be kind.

———————

*God, You are kind to me. Help me to show Your kindness to oth-
ers, even when it is undeserved. Lord, I can't do that on my own!
Fill me with Your Spirit and give me grace to show kindness.*

WEDNESDAY

*He stationed the gatekeepers at the gates of
the house of the LORD so that no one should
enter who was in any way unclean.*
2 Chronicles 23:19

The ancient Chinese built their great wall as a protection from their enemies to the north. The wall was too high, too thick, and too long to be breached in any way. But within a hundred years of the wall's completion, China was invaded! Unfortunately, the character of the gatekeeper wasn't as strong as the wall.

You are the gatekeeper of your own heart. If there are breaches in your character, the enemy can advance in your life. God will keep you safe and secure when you are a faithful guard over your heart. Walk in holiness and build a life of godly character. That will keep the enemy out.

Lord, help me to guard my heart and to live in integrity and holiness before You. Give me grace to walk close to You so that my life is clean and brings honor to Jesus Christ.

Thursday

When I am afraid, I put my trust in you.
Psalm 56:3

Recently I was experiencing really bothersome physical symptoms. My heart raced, I had shortness of breath. My mouth dried up and my muscles were tense. I had a terrible time trying to concentrate, and my mind just raced all the time. I wasn't ill; I was afraid! I was facing a real fear, and I felt sick.

It's unavoidable: at times we will be afraid. As you deliberately and intentionally take your fearful situation and the people involved and place them by faith in the Lord's hands, and as you trust Him to take care of everything, He will relieve your fears. If you are fearful today, bring everything you're afraid of to the Lord. He will give you courage.

Lord, You are greater than anything that causes me fear; help me to live like I believe that! When fear comes, give me Your grace to trust You so that I can enjoy Your peace.

Friday

And an angel of the Lord appeared to them,
and the glory of the Lord shone around them,
and they were filled with great fear.

Luke 2:9

In 1882, the very first strand of Christmas lights – just eight lights costing about $100 in today's money - were put on a Christmas tree. It started a trend that continues today. Now we have lights on our trees, on our bushes, and on the roof. Maybe the Christmas lights from your neighbor's house keep you up all night. Even the tiniest light can bring all kinds of light to darkness.

The Bible says that when the angel of the Lord appeared, the glory of God, his light, shone in every direction. Why was the light shining? Because the light of the world, Jesus Christ, had come. Wherever Jesus is there is light, and the darkness has to flee.

Lord Jesus, I praise You that sin and darkness have no place where You are because You are the light of the world. Thank you that sin and darkness have no place in me, because you live in me.

SATURDAY

And in the same region there were shepherds out in the field, keeping watch over their flock by night.

Luke 2:8

Most of us don't know what complete, black darkness looks like at night. However, shepherds in the fields experience thick, inky, black darkness where you can see nothing at all. If you're a shepherd and it's your birthday, that doesn't sound like much of a place to celebrate.

Someone has said that if you take Christ out of Christmas, December would be bleak and colorless. But because Jesus came, this season is filled with joy! Jesus shows up for His own birthday, bringing light to the darkness, and He brings all the presents. He brings the gifts of peace, of joy, and of salvation. And that makes for a wonderful, joyful celebration.

Lord Jesus, I praise You for the joy that is mine because You were born. Lord, I pray for those who are living in darkness to receive Your gift of salvation so they can know Your great joy.

SUNDAY

For unto you is born this day in the city
of David a Savior, who is Christ the Lord.

Luke 2:11

Most of us would say that Christmas began the day Jesus was born. But it actually started long before that, in the heart of God. Though from the beginning of creation we have sinned and fallen short of God's glory, He still loves us. He knew that the only sacrifice that could remove our sin was the blood of His Son Jesus. Christmas was set in motion long before Jesus was born.

Christmas is only complete when it changes your heart! Jesus Christ wants to transform your heart and give you His gift of eternal life. Today, God promises to save you when you call on Him and ask for His gift of salvation.

God, Thank You for the gift of Your Son Jesus Christ to die in my place to forgive my sin. I believe he rose from the dead to give me eternal life. Jesus, I trust in You to save me. Thank You, Jesus!

Monday

And Mary said to the angel,
"How will this be, since I am a virgin?"
Luke 1:34

I don't understand how a combustion engine works. Yet for all of my life I've traveled successfully in cars with combustion engines. I don't understand how a microwave works; yet I use one to warm up my cold coffee. We trust things we don't really understand all the time.

It is difficult to understand the virgin birth – not even Mary understood it! It's not necessary to understand it to believe it. It was necessary for Jesus Christ to be born of a virgin. Otherwise, He would have inherited the sin nature that we have. Because Jesus was born of a virgin, He was born without sin. Only a sinless Savior can save sinners.

Father, I don't understand all of Your ways, but I don't
have to. Lord, thank You that Jesus was born of a virgin so
I could be saved. I believe You and I trust Jesus to save me.
Thank You, God!

TUESDAY

She will bear a son, and you shall call his name
Jesus, for he will save his people from their sins.
Matthew 1:21

A great responsibility of parents is choosing their child's name. They might consider family names, biblical names, or popular names. Maybe the names of sports heroes or movie stars make the list. If an angel comes and gives you the name of the child, you don't need a name list. You just name the child what the angel says!

The name Jesus is a saving name. Everything about who Jesus is and what He has done is wrapped up in His name. The Bible says, "Everyone who believes in Him receives forgiveness of sins through His name." His is a beautiful name and the only name that saves.

Lord Jesus, how I Thank You for Your mission to save me from my sin. Jesus, help me to lift up Your name to everyone around me so they can also know Your beautiful name and be saved.

Wednesday

Which he will display at the proper time—
he who is the blessed and only Sovereign, the
King of kings and Lord of lords.
1 Timothy 6:15

My wife Michele beautifully decorates our home for Christmas with Nativity sets throughout our house. In each one of the Nativity sets, Jesus is small and everybody else is big. Of course, that's fitting. It would be very strange if the baby was huge and everybody else was small.

Sometimes we try to keep Jesus small. We want to be big and in charge of our own lives, keeping Jesus small and on the margins, reserved for Sundays and times of crisis. The Lord Jesus Christ is the King of heaven and earth. He was born a tiny child in a humble place, but He reigns as the Sovereign. He deserves to be Lord and King of your life.

Lord Jesus, You were introduced to the world as a tiny baby, but
You are the King of all kings and the Lord of all! I pray that
You would have rule over every part of my life.

THURSDAY

But as he considered these things, behold, an angel of
the Lord appeared to him in a dream, saying, "Joseph,
son of David, do not fear to take Mary as your wife, for
that which is conceived in her is from the Holy Spirit."

Matthew 1:20

A child wakened by a loud storm ran to his parents' room. He knocked loudly at the door and called out, "It's storming! Can I get in bed with you?" They welcomed him into their room. He crawled under the covers, snuggled close to his dad, and quickly fell asleep – not because his dad somehow calmed the storm, but because of his dad's presence.

God does not always quiet the storms that rage around us. But He always is present with us in the midst of them. The angel assured Joseph that his and Mary's daunting circumstance was God's plan. Joseph was not alone. God was with him, and he didn't have to be afraid. God's nearness is all we need to calm our fears.

God, Thank You for being as near to me as You were to Joseph.
Thank You for being present in my trials so that I don't have to
fear. Help me to stay close to you when I am afraid.

FRIDAY

And he was transfigured before them, and his face shone like the sun, and his clothes became white as light.
Matthew 17:2

Recently we shopped for a plant to decorate our porch. Michele chose this scrawny, faded mum. I trust my wife's plant skills, but I didn't trust that mum. It was sad looking – not pretty. But Michele watered, and fed, and nursed that plant, until one day, that mum was bursting with blooms. Its beauty had always been there, but it hadn't yet been revealed.

When Jesus came to earth, His glory was concealed. Born in a cattle stall, raised in obscurity, humiliated, and killed on a criminal's cross – there's not much glory there. But to those who believe Him, He not only reveals His glory; He transforms us to reflect His glory more and more.

Lord Jesus, Thank You for revealing Your glory to us. O Lord, as I spend time with You, transform me into Your image so others may see You in me. Use me, Lord, to show Your glory!

SATURDAY

Then he said to them, "But who do you say that I am?" And Peter answered, "The Christ of God."
Luke 9:20

Media mogul Ted Turner once famously offered his opinion of Jesus Christ. He said that Jesus was a loser and that Christianity is a religion for losers. A devout Muslim will tell you that Jesus is the greatest prophet. Others say that Jesus isn't real, but a legend, like King Arthur. Just about everyone has an opinion about Jesus.

But who do you say Jesus is? Do you know that Jesus Christ is real, that He is God's Son, and that He died on the cross to pay for your sin? He rose from the dead to give you eternal life. Jesus Christ is the only one who saves, and He will save you if you will put your faith in Him today!

Jesus, You are the Son of God. You are Lord of my life. You are the one true God; I can follow no one else. I pray for people I know and love to put their faith in You.

SUNDAY

*For to this you have been called, because Christ
also suffered for you, leaving you an example,
so that you might follow in his steps.*
1 Peter 2:21

As a young child my dad took me to play in a creek. Dad would say, "Stephen, watch; I'm going to step on that stone, and that stone, and that stone. Then you step where I step and follow me. You can do it." When the steps were harder, he took my hand and helped me. And when the steps became too big, he'd carry me across the creek.

God guides us like that, going ahead and showing us where to step. He knows when to take our hand and help us. And when the steps are too big for us to handle, He carries us. We follow God by faith, but we never walk alone.

————————

God, Thank You that Jesus has shown me how to walk. He's the light of the world, and Your Word is a lamp for my feet and a light to my path. Help me to walk in his steps every day.

MONDAY

This is God, our God forever and ever.
He will guide us forever.
Psalm 48:14

An aircraft pilot following a highway below saw a vehicle repeatedly attempting to pass a semi-truck on a two-lane road. The truck blocked his vision. So the driver would veer out to look around the truck, and then move back when he couldn't pass safely. He repeated this maneuver several times. The pilot thought, "I can see everything he can't see. If only I could tell that driver what I see, he could pass that truck safely."

God has perfect knowledge of what's ahead of you. As you stay close to Him through His Word and prayer, ask His Holy Spirit to guide you, He will guide you safely today, tomorrow, and for the rest of your life.

O Lord, You are my faithful guide through life. Following You, I can never lose my way. Holy Spirit, fill me and guide me today in every situation. Help me have confidence as I walk with You.

TUESDAY

For the Lamb in the midst of the throne will be their shepherd, and he will guide them to springs of living water, and God will wipe away every tear from their eyes.
Revelation 7:17

Two adventurers planning a trip to the Andes Mountains went to visit Elisabeth Eliot, who knew the area very well. They were perhaps overly confident, and asked few questions. All they wanted from Elisabeth was a few phrases that would help them communicate with the native people. Elisabeth Eliot wrote this: "So often we think all we need is a road sign, or a map, or a few phrases. But what we really need is a guide – someone who knows the way."

Jesus not only knows the way; He is the way. When we walk with Him we may not know where we're going next. But we don't have to. He knows the way, and He faithfully guides us wherever He wants to take us.

———

Lord Jesus, You are my faithful Shepherd. You've not called me to know what's ahead, but to simply follow You. You know the way I should go; help me to stay close to You as You lead me.

WEDNESDAY

For those whom he foreknew he also predestined to be conformed to the image of his Son, in order that he might be the firstborn among many brothers.

Romans 8:29

A drill sergeant was asked how he took raw recruits of all kinds and turned them into good Marines. He said, "It's really simple. On the first day of boot camp, I have a vision for every recruit. I know how I want them to walk and to talk. I know how I want them to think. And I work on them until my vision for them becomes a reality."

God's vision for you is that you walk, talk, and think like Jesus Christ. Everything He does in your life is to make that vision a reality. As you follow Him, you will be transformed from an immature believer into a Christ-like man or woman.

God, Thank You that You have created me and saved me with a good purpose in mind, planned out from the beginning! Thank You for transforming my life to make me like Jesus.

Thursday

And my God will supply every need of yours
according to his riches in glory in Christ Jesus.
Philippians 4:19

You can count out loud to ten, or a hundred, or even to a thousand. But if you kept counting, it will take longer than you've got to reach a million. Then a billion is a thousand times that. And a trillion is a thousand times that. Those numbers are beyond our ability to count, but they're real, measurable numbers.

God's riches are immeasurable. He's able to give you all you need to be what He wants you to be, and the ability to do what He wants you to do. He generously gives to us, not *out* of His riches, but *according* to His riches. Trust Him, and you will lack for nothing you really need.

Lord God, You've promised to meet my needs according to Your riches because I'm Your child. Thank You that I don't need to beg or worry; You always provide generously for Your children!

FRIDAY

*Fear not, for I am with you; be not dismayed, for
I am your God; I will strengthen you, I will help you,
I will uphold you with my righteous right hand.*
Isaiah 41:10

Once when I was on a crowded airport train, I was standing, holding onto the vertical bar to steady myself. A young mother holding a baby boarded the train. She held to the same bar I held to. After a moment her baby reached over to the bar and put his hand on it, just like his mother. I thought, "I wonder if he thinks he's holding himself up?" Obviously, that baby's stability didn't depend on his own strength.

Just as that baby was held by the mother's strength, God holds you up. He not only strengthens you; He is your strength! So whatever He asks of you, you can do it, because God can, and He lives in you.

---

*Lord God, You have promised to be with me, to
strengthen me, to help me, and to hold me up. I don't need
to worry, but to rest in Your faithful care. Thank You for
committing to take care of me!*

SATURDAY

Oh, how abundant is your goodness, which you have stored up for those who fear you and worked for those who take refuge in you, in the sight of the children of mankind!

Psalm 31:19

At the candy store, the owner, Mr. Johnson held a huge container of lollipops down to Billy. He said, "Hey buddy, reach in here and grab some lollipops – as many as you can hold." Billy didn't move. Finally, Mr. Johnson grabbed a fistful of lollipops, and gave them to Billy. Billy's mom said, "Son, why wouldn't you reach in for the lollipops?" Billy said, "Because Mr. Johnsons' hands are a lot bigger than mine!"

God stores up His goodness for those who fear Him! He blesses abundantly when we come to Him with hands empty and open, asking Him to fill them. He is able to give you more than you can even imagine from His abundant goodness.

Father, Thank You for Your goodness to me in Jesus Christ! Help me to show others how good and kind You are so they can know You.

CPSIA information can be obtained
at www.ICGtesting.com
Printed in the USA
BVHW040538070723
666618BV00002B/4

9 781953 331229